SKIING FREESTYLE

SKIING FREESTYLE

Official Training Guide of the U.S. Freestyle Ski Team

Park Smalley and Hilary Engisch

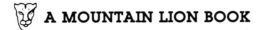 A MOUNTAIN LION BOOK

Taylor Publishing Company
Dallas, Texas

Be aware that following instructions in this book
could involve physical risk, even though every effort
has been made in the preparation of this book to stress
the need for safety consciousness and proper technique.

Photographs by Hilary Engisch on pages
6, 126, 134, 141, 146, 163, 169 and 172–173.

Library of Congress Cataloging-in-Publication Data

Smalley, Park.
    Skiing freestyle.

    1. Skis and skiing—United States—Training.
I. Engisch, Hilary.   II. Title.
GV854.85.S63   1985   796.93'07073   85-25104

ISBN 0-87833-520-X
Printed in the United States of America

0 9 8 7 6 5 4 3 2 1

BOOK DESIGN BY LURELLE CHEVERIE

Contents

Acknowledgments

Hardly any book published today is the sole creation of its author. This book is no exception. In fact, *Skiing Freestyle* is much more, because it is a part of a growing phenomenon in publishing—book producing. Which is simply the creation, development and production of a book by a source outside the publishing house. *Skiing Freestyle* was produced by Mountain Lion, Inc., an independent book producer that specializes in sports, health, fitness and professional books.

To bring a book to fruition, a producer relies on many persons, each with something special to contribute. And so, we thank you, one and all.

- *Jon Naso*, photographer of Sports Action Photography, who took nearly all the photographs.
- *Bob Frese*, editor of Taylor Publishing, who shepherded the manuscript.
- *Mary Horwath*, former director of the U.S. Freestyle Ski Team, who provided logistical support.

Also: Jan Bucher, Lane Spina, Seth Goldsmith, Peter Cure, Kris Fedderson, Krista Pettibone and all the members of the U.S. Freestyle Ski Team; the Paul Graves Family, Jack Fleming, Jean Kiedaisch, Randy Bergey, Anita Ackerly; Lisa Fernandez and Roger Bryant of the University of Vermont; Dr. Robert Engisch, Josh Clemmons, Kevin Clayton, John Evans, Gail LeBaron, James and Robert Quinn, Paul Nicholas, Jay Simpson; Matt Bryzcki of Rutgers University and Lorrie Hones, Greg March and the Princeton Nautilus Center; Joanne and Werner Frentop and Vinnie Hermanson of the Langhorne Ski Shop; the Killington Ski Area, Bolton Valley Ski Area, Yamaha Ski Company and all the kids from the Vermont Ski Training Foundation.

John J. Monteleone
Mountain Lion Inc.
Rocky Hill, N.J.
June, 1985

With much love to my parents,
Joan-Pryse and Robert,
who have been a constant inspiration
to me from the time I was young,
and to the Paul Graves family,
whose laughter and gracious
kindness I shall never forget.

HILARY A. ENGISCH

CHAPTER 1

Freestyle Skiing

Humans have always been playful and curious. Playing is as natural to a child as breathing. And it has been said that a child can ask more questions in a minute than a philosopher can deal with in a lifetime. Lucky is the adult who can retain this light and curious spirit and incorporate it into his work. Without these two traits, we would become woefully predictable . . . and many a new frontier would go undiscovered. Certainly freestyle, the young relative of alpine skiing, would not have developed but for that spirit. Intrepid racers asked "What if . . ." and then tried. Those first few steps have freed the skier from the sometimes closed, staunch, narrow-minded "correct" way of doing things advocated by many ski school and racing programs: that is, to be an expert skier you MUST run gates, you MUST stand only on the inside edge of the downhill ski, you MUST stay on the snow, you MUST face forward. These traditional ideas went unchallenged from the late

My father always used to tell me, "Paul, at a moment in which you feel indispensible, take a glass of water, stick your finger in it, and upon pulling it out see how much of a dent you leave."

PAUL GRAVES

1800s to the early 1900s. But, again, the human race is a playful and curious lot, and these ideas were bound to be questioned.

Questioned they were. By 1929, Dr. Fritz Reuel, a European who invented the Reuel Christi in ballet skiing, was experimenting with pole flips and spins. Under his influence, skiers started to transfer their individual talents from the gymnastic sports halls and the ice rinks onto the ski slopes. They began to experiment with spins, jumps, and pole flips, which is all the more surprising when you consider that these new tricks were attempted on 210 cm skis! Ballet was born!

Skiers like Stein Eriksen, a former Olympic gold medalist in alpine racing and a maverick who fancied the unexpected, explored the possibility of going upside down on skis and landing on their feet. Eriksen, one of the first freestyle judges, brought aerials to the attention of enthusiastic skiers by performing front layouts just for fun. This led to aerial shows in Sun Valley, Idaho, in the 1950s. Doug Pfeiffer, then the editor of *Skiing Magazine,* envisioned a type of skiing which broke all the rules. Picking up on Eriksen's lead, between 1956 and 1962 Pfeiffer taught tricks like the Charleston, the worm turn, and the kickback in "The School of Exotic Skiing." At the same time, when out of the bamboo, top alpine racers spent their time training on the flats and the unforgiving terrain of the mogul slope. They discovered that a different technique was required to tame "the bumps," and changed their style to fit the demands of the slope.

Freestyle, like its name, grew haphazardly from roughly 1929 until the early 1970s. While ski techniques were changing, some basic human qualities remained constant: athletes, from the beginning of time, have thrived on comparison, and it was only a matter of years before aerial, ballet, and mogul skiers were watching each other, sizing each other up, trying to outdo one another. The next step, naturally, was to design a forum in which they could compete. In 1966, Peter Pinkham staged a new and very different type of ski competition, "The Masters Tour." At Killington, Glen Ellen (now Sugarbush North), and Stratton Mountain in Vermont, champions like Herman Goeller and Tom Leroy performed inverted aerials and ballet routines, and skied the moguls. Throughout the late 1960s athletes such as Suzy Chaffee and Corkey Fowler demonstrated increasingly difficult tricks.

But it wasn't until 1971 that ballet, aerial, and mogul skiing became more formalized when Waterville Valley Ski Area in New Hampshire held the National Championships of Exhibition Skiing. (The term freestyle hadn't yet evolved.) Here, amateurs and professionals competed against each other in all three events, which were combined into one run. Imagine sailing off three consecutive aerial jumps without a break, then dropping directly into a mogul field, skiing that until

Hermann Reitberger—GRB, Richard Schabl—GRB, Lane Spina—U.S.A.

you reach the flats, then ending with a complete ballet routine!

Meanwhile in the West, the Rocky Mountain Professional Freestyle Championships were held. In this competition the one-run format was dropped and the three events were run separately, setting the standards for future competitive events. But the sport still needed a sanctioned and universally accepted name. Later this year the all inclusive term "Freestyle Skiing" was coined by Doug Pfeiffer and Tom Corcoran (director of skiing at Waterville Valley); the sport was on its way.

But what were the criteria for these events and how were individual performances scored? Performances in all three events were judged and points were awarded in each discipline. The athlete holding the highest score placed first. In aerials, the skier was judged on the degree of difficulty of the jump, form in the air, and landing. The distance and height of the jump, too, contributed to the overall score. In the ballet event, the judges looked for degree of difficulty, fluidity, grace, and eventually choreography once Suzie Chaffee introduced music to the sport. Through the 1960s and 1970s the mogul event was judged more on sheer excitement than technical skill. However, the jumps and speed that played such an important role at that time eventually led to more sophisticated judging criteria. Today, judges look for a style which incorporates the technical perfection of setting the ski on edge, as it's designed to be used, in a carved turn.

There is no sound but your breath and the pounding of a heart, no sight, but of a white swath of snow, and no memory, save that you were once ready. This is the calm in the eye of the competitive storm . . . an addiction which you will come to both fear and love.

HILARY ENGISCH

With a judging and event format in effect by 1972, freestyle competitions began flourishing around the country. They were immediately popular with the American public; the events were self-governed, extremely social, and appealed to the free and easy spirit. Its athletes were young, fit daredevils whose fearlessness and self-sufficient natures made them easily idealized. The media helped supply the public with "heroes" and visions of the "small town girl who makes good," which is so appealing to the American imagination. Still, these events retained the sense of challenge, fierce yet friendly competition, and freedom within limitations, which played a part in the popularity of the sport.

At first, each event was scored in increments of .5 out of a possible 20. Later, thanks to U.S. international judge Paul Nicholas, the 10 point scale was introduced, easing point tabulation. At the same time, the U.S. Ski Association created a Freestyle Committee, and published a freestyle rule book. The sport was changing. Music was introduced to ballet skiing by Chaffee in 1973, and Marion and Ellen Post set new standards in aerial competition for women by performing inverted aerials for the first time in 1974. From 1974 until 1980, both professional and amateur freestyle developed side by side, with the more advanced freestyle skiers like Scotty Brooksbank, Wayne Wong, Suzie Chaffee, Genia Fuller, and Marion and Ellen Post competing on the pro tours.

Things began to take off in the freestyle world in 1975 when Colgate and Midas sponsored tours with prize money worth $90,000 and $125,000, respectively. Genia Fuller and Mark Steigemeier became Freestyle Skiers of the Year; within five years the sport and its athletes had burst into the limelight. Meanwhile, the national amateur championships were held for the first time at Killington, Vermont; the two top young hopefuls were Bruce Bolesky and Karen Colburn.

In 1976, a professional World Cup Tour began and international competition became part of the sport, with U.S. competitors traveling to Canada and Europe. At the same time another tour, The Chevy Tour, began in the United States under the auspices of the American Freestyle Skiers Association. The two tours were at odds in the sense that they were running simultaneously, both trying to attract the best athletes, and both trying to claim that their skiers were the best in the United States. The Professional Freestyle Association (PFA) won out, becoming the only tour in existence by 1977.

In 1978 and 1979, securing underwriters for the inverted aerial event became difficult, and the tour was forced to stage all of its events in Canada and Europe. If it weren't for resourceful athletes like Scotty Brooksbank, who started the Freestyle Skiers of America

(FSA), professional freestyle would have disappeared altogether. Despite serious internal turmoil caused by insurance problems, during May of 1979 the Congress of Le Federation International de Ski (FIS), ski administrators, and freestyle athletes from around the world met in London to discuss recognizing freestyle skiing as an official event along with the likes of alpine and nordic ski racing.

World Cup Freestyle returned to the U.S. in 1980 for an event at the Pocono Mountains in Pennsylvania. This was significant because, for the first time in two years, American athletes would be allowed to compete in their own country. Eyes were fixed upon the aerial event; organizers paid great attention to detail, and the competition was a success. Freestyle, and most importantly, the aerial event, were back. When the FIS committee approved the sport in 1980–1981, former

**As soon as you trust yourself,
you will know how to live.**

GOETHE

professional athletes were given the option of turning amateur and joining the U.S. Freestyle Ski Team. In 1981 many former professional athletes, including Jan Bucher, Bruce Bolesky, Hilary Engisch, and Frank Beddor III, were granted amateur status and became part of the first official U.S. Freestyle Ski Team. The sport had taken its first step toward becoming an Olympic event.

From 1980 to the present, The World Cup Tour has been going strong in North America and Europe. The addition of teams from as far away as Sweden, Japan, and Australia reflects the sport's reemergence and growing popularity. In 1988 freestyle skiing will debut in the Calgary Winter Olympics as a demonstration

sport, bringing freestyle back into the public eye on a large scale for the first time since the 1970s.

Sometimes the chanciest of discoveries, the accidents, are the first threads of a fine fabric. In sport, you may be uncertain of what you are capable of attaining, or of where this challenge will take you. But the intrigue of this thing called "potential" stirs an unquenchable thirst in everyone involved with freestyle.

The qualities inherent in the building of a sport's tradition, its customs, code of ethics, rules, and competition formats, as well as the curious, playful nature of this country's people were responsible for freestyle's emergence in the early 1900s. These traits are ever present today. They can be found at each event and are

Steve Desovitch—U.S.A. and Jan Bucher—U.S.A.

Nineteen members of the Sunset Sports Center's "Hot Dog" team at Grand Targhee Ski Resort, Wyoming, performed a simultaneous back flip while holding hands on February 9, 1975.

Guinness Book of World Records

the driving force behind the endless work of the organizers, the love of the parents, the sense of wonder in the crowd, and the nervous laughter of both coach and competitor.

Behind this work, love, wonder, and laughter is a certainty, a confidence that we ourselves make things happen, and that much is possible. That dreams are not mere whims of idle men. That chance takes hold now and again, sometimes leading us by the coattails. And thankfully so. That it's possible to turn things around, and that dreams do come true. One has simply to take the chance. In many ways, freestyle skiing is *the* American sport.

The sport is ready . . . because its athletes have the stuff of which discoveries are made.

CHAPTER 2

The Moguls

Do you remember
How you won that last race . . .?
How you flung your body
At the start . . .

Do you remember . . .?
Don't you think
I lurched with you . . .?

And when you flew into the stretch
Was not all my thrill
Of a thousand races
In your blood
At your final drive
Through the finish line . . .?

Look straight ahead
Think only of the goal
Run high
Run hard

Save nothing
And finish
With an ecstatic burst . . .

FRANK HORNE

Work consists of whatever a body is *obliged* to do . . . Play consists of whatever a body is not obliged to do.

MARK TWAIN

Of the three events which comprise freestyle skiing, the mogul event is the most intimately tied to downhill skiing. For a good alpine skier interested in perfecting technique or in competing, mogul skiing becomes an attractive answer for a number of reasons. When you train skiing moguls, you get to ski, and ski, and ski . . . from the top of the mountain to the bottom. You are not confined to the practice slope for the day, running bamboo, nor are you limited to learning a turning technique which is specific to one type of skiing. If you learn how to ski the moguls, you'll be able to transfer your expertise to just about any natural ski terrain. This is a skill you'll have for the rest of your life, not just while you're competing.

The moguls are the most directly competitive of the three events; it's much less of a performance than the ballet, which is choreographed, or the aerial event, in which it's just your body and the air. The moguls pit skier against skier directly, without pomp or ceremony. But it's more than that . . . it's skier against that anonymous master, the mountain, whose runs are impossible to plan. For try as you may to memorize his terrain, when it comes to that final push through the starting wand, the body becomes a twitch of action-reaction, at the mercy of an ever changing terrain, at an ever increasing speed. When all you can remember is a blur of colorful motion the decision-making is instantaneous and unrelenting . . . one turn—into another—into another. And then, so quickly, it's over.

You are reduced to 45 seconds. Forty-five seconds to prove yourself, to put it all together. All those hours —no, years—of training, compressed into moments, only to be given a numerical value. It's exhausting, nerve-wracking. And if you are to be one of the best athletes in the starting gate, you've got to want to go, want the pressure, the chance to ski the run . . . but this time, in 44 seconds.

The Moguls

Skimming this chapter, you may be surprised to find that the first half of the instructional material on skiing moguls takes place on terrain without moguls. This is not an oversight . . . there's a method behind this madness! A pianist must develop dexterity and strength in his fingers before he is able to play a more difficult piece. A skier, too, must approach learning in a similar fashion, breaking down the parts of the turn, working on individual problems on flat terrain before trying to orchestrate the whole turn.

This chapter assumes that you are, at the very least, an intermediate skier. The exercises on the flats are useful drills for improving intermediate and advanced techniques, so don't make the mistake of assuming you can just breeze over them if you're only having problems on expert terrain. You've got to learn how the correct technique feels under controlled conditions, and on terrain that reduces outside variables. This will enable you to pinpoint problems. Take the time to analyze your technique on flat terrain, preferably with another person who can critique your progress. To begin, let's look at some ski terminology.

Definitions

THE FALLINE—is the most direct path down the mountain. If you were to place a ball at the top of a ski slope and let the force of gravity and the natural slope of the trail guide it downhill, it would roll down the falline. Ideally, a mogul slope should have a falline that drops straight down the trail. A straight falline is a pleasure to ski; you can weight your turns equally, face squarely down the slope, and develop a rhythm by skiing pitches at a time. While the best mogul trails have straight fallines, it's not uncommon to find some trails that are cut against a natural falline, and are higher on one side than the other. In this case, the falline runs from the high side to the low side of the trail. Skiing directly down this falline leads you into the woods. To prevent this, you have to fight the slope or pull one turn in tighter than the other.

THE MOGUL LINE—so often referred to by skiers, is the straight path between two alternating rows of moguls that you see if you look down a mogul slope. The sides of the moguls create a trough which descends the mogul field, usually straight down the falline. This trough is the line that you should try to ski down by setting the ski on edge to turn and slicing through the snow, carving the ski along the side of the mogul. These edge sets on the side of the mogul line will push, or rebound, the skis into the next turn, making it possible to keep turning in a very tight trough.

ABSORPTION—is when a skier bends the knees while holding the upper body square. It's one of the most important techniques in mogul skiing. By bending the knees to accommodate the contour of the slope, you can keep your upper body "quiet," and your skis on the snow, even if the terrain is very irregular. When a mogul skier absorbs a bump, the skis appear as if they're snaking along the snow. This helps you keep your balance. When absorbing, the ski can lie flat on the snow, or on edge. After bending the knees to accommodate a mogul you then extend the legs. This higher stance enables you to keep your ski in contact with the snow, and also to begin another turn.

EXTENSION—occurs at the end of a mogul turn. As mentioned, during absorption the knees are bent and brought up toward the chest at the high point of the mogul or trough. You actually suck the irregularity in the slope up with the knees. As the bump drops away into the trough, the knees and legs extend, "pushing" away from the mogul. Think of absorption as "coiling" the legs up, and of extension as "uncoiling" the legs. There will be brief moments when your skis will leave the snow, but they contour to the angle of the slope if your knees are bent and upper body position is square. By pressing down the back side of the mogul you can keep the skis in contact with the snow throughout most of the turn, making your technique smooth and balanced. As you extend the legs, you begin to set the skis on edge into the next turn.

EDGING OR "CARVING"—a ski makes it possible to turn without sliding. Technically, it is the most efficient way to initiate a turn. To place a ski on edge you must

Absorbtion

incline the knees up "into" the hill, and weight the downhill ski. When carving the ski edge, you can feel it slice through the snow, and grab securely on icy terrain. Edging should begin at the tip of the ski, with weight continuing smoothly from tip to tail. In the moguls, edging occurs primarily during extension.

STAYING SQUARE—means that the upper body faces down the hill throughout the turn. In other words, the upper body stays perpendicular to the falline, while the knees and skis cross back and forth over the falline, carving the ski through the turn.

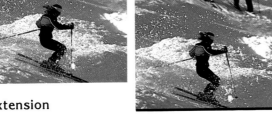

Extension

Agility Exercises on Flat Terrain— Tuning Your Technique

Regardless of your ability, practicing the following exercises on the flats can help you tune your ski technique. Even if you are an expert skier, you should look through these drills, go out on the flats, and train with them . . . they're fun as well as challenging.

If you are a skier caught in a wide track parallel, either on the flats or in the moguls, it could be for a number of reasons. One possibility is that you're placing too much weight on the uphill ski, which prevents it from sliding in next to the downhill ski. You can practice several steps to work through this stage. If you are an intermediate skier, you are probably used to sliding your skis around through the turn without much concern about edging. But to mogul ski correctly, you must put the ski on edge. The best place to learn, or to practice, is on the flats.

Let's review the beginning turn, and then try some drills to help you improve your technique. But first, consider the following basic stance of an intermediate skier:

The basic ski stance on flat terrain, whether it be wide or closed track parallel, is somewhat higher than on steeper slopes, with the legs a little straighter. As you progress through this chapter and try these drills on increasingly steep terrain, you will need to bend the knees more, but for the moment it should look like this:

- The head is centered between the shoulders, and held comfortably.
- The arms are bent slightly at the elbow and raised up and out.
- The hips face forward squarely and are dropped down slightly as the knees bend.
- The feet are placed shoulder width apart if you are an intermediate skier, a bit closer if you are

Intermediate and Advanced Technique

an advanced skier, with weight primarily on the downhill ski.

With this stance you're probably able to make a turn on flat terrain which is smooth, despite either a sliding ski or weight placed equally on both skis. On the flats you can get away with these mistakes—not so in the moguls. This basic stance is a guideline, but don't think of it as the Bible. You should be relaxed and able to adapt quickly to changes in terrain. But if you were to hold your arms just so, at 10 and two o'clock while skiing, and stand on the edge just so at all times, you would be tense, and your technique would look stilted and unnatural. In addition, you'd be unable to react to the sudden changes in the slope which always occur. Skiers have different styles, and no one way of standing on the skis is right for all individuals, but there are a few basics. Try to keep these in mind, but most of all . . . relax.

Problems with the Basic Wide Track Sliding Turn

The basic wide track sliding turn is fine as a learning tool for mastering the carve turn. Unfortunately, many people get caught in this, never quite developing the ability to put the ski on the downhill inside edge as it's designed to be used. If you tend to slide the ski through the turn, putting weight on both skis equally, it's difficult to go on to skiing moguls correctly, and a host of balance problems begin to rear their ugly heads. You may end up compensating for a lack of technique by twisting the upper body, or turning on the tail of the ski. In any case, you develop bad habits.

In a wide track sliding turn the skier usually makes a long approach, steering into the falline either by stemming as shown here, or by sliding on the base of the ski at the beginning of the turn, and then placing equal weight on both skis halfway through the turn. There is very little bend or inclination of the knees. The wide track sliding turn looks something like this:

parts separately, exaggerating the movements in drills first before putting everything back together. Each turn is made up of the following parts: the approach and anticipation of the turn, the edge set/down-weighting, the pole plant, up-weighting/rebounding, and the transfer of weight onto the new downhill ski edge.

Breaking the Wide Track through Exaggeration

Approach, Anticipation with Edge Set

Approach and anticipation occur at the beginning of every turn, whether it be a giant slalom, slalom, mogul, or intermediate recreational turn. The approach is a neutral body position; it's the point between the end of one turn and the beginning of the next when the body is light. For the intermediate skier, the approach is sometimes a traverse. For an expert skier, it is a balance point in which the body is uncommitted or able to turn in either direction as the skier travels straight down the falline. If you're skiing in a wide track parallel, your neutral body position will be similar to the basic stance mentioned above. The only difference is that you will be moving across, or down the hill.

If you are skiing in a closed parallel, your legs and skis will be held closer together, but your upper body position is that of the basic stance outlined above.

Anticipation is a change in body position from the approach which helps initiate the turn. It sets the lower body up for a change in direction. To anticipate the turn, drop the hips and bend the knees while simultaneously pushing the tails of the skis "away" from you just a hair. At the same time, you should look down the slope, into the falline. Both of these things help place pressure on the downhill ski. Also, by pushing the downhill ski away from your body, it will automatically be placed on its inside edge a little! If you let the uphill ski remain light and slide it into the downhill ski, you can get rid of the wide stance. You'll feel the ski grab a bit, and it's at this point that you should drop your weight into the edge set and plant the pole. Try this in a drill:

If an intermediate skier is stemming, that's good, because it means that for an instant he is on the downhill ski completely. If the skier then weights both skis heavily, it's next to impossible to arch or carve a turn. Instead, the skier skids in a wide stance. In the moguls you would be out-of-control in three turns!

To progress beyond this point, it's sometimes helpful to break the turn down into parts and practice these

Let your skis glide down the hill, begin to push the tails away from the body, keeping the uphill ski light. Turn the knees up into the hill as you drop your weight onto the downhill ski and plant the pole. Exaggerate the edge set so that it is abrupt, making your weight drop quickly.

The Pole Plant

The pole plant occurs at the same time the edge is set during anticipation, and it makes possible the up-weighting necessary to steer the skis into the next turn. You can tell a great deal by the way a skier plants a pole. A passive skier will plant the pole lazily with a limp wrist, which makes the lower arm turn out away from the body. This can force the shoulders back and break balance to the rear. At the other extreme, a tense skier will plant the poles too close to the body, almost shrugging the shoulders and certainly tensing the back. Likewise, planting the poles out to the side also occurs when a skier is tense and preoccupied with form instead of function. And someone who does not use the poles at all develops a host of problems! Unable to initiate a turn by unweighting, this skier usually compensates by swinging the upper body and hips in the direction of the new turn.

The pole plant should be strong and dynamic. As

the edges are set and the hips drop, the pole is placed in the snow halfway between the tip of the ski and the toe of the boot. You should reach for the pole plant as seen here. This "reaching" helps keep the upper body facing down the falline. A skier who appears to shrug away from a turn and who plants the pole hesitantly is probably frightened. By reaching, you're committing yourself to the turn; you are ready both physically and mentally.

Rebounding into and across the Falline

The grabbing sensation from the edges biting into the snow is what will begin to rebound you into and across the falline. (Rebounding becomes extremely important when you take this drill into the moguls.) The more weight you drop onto the downhill ski as it's pushed away from the body during anticipation, the less the ski will slide, and the more power you can transfer across the falline.

If you're having trouble putting all of these steps together, try this drill across the hill. For instance, from a traverse drop down into the approach, set the edge as you drop the hips down over your boots, and plant the pole. Then release the weight from your edges, take a high stance, and begin the drill again. Do this eight times in each direction. Concentrate on going from a high stance to a low one, and remember to place more pressure on the downhill ski edge.

The next step is to steer your skis across the falline. To do this, lighten the pressure placed on the ski edges during anticipation by straightening the knees a little immediately after the edge grabs in the snow. As the edges release, turn your hips into the falline. A short push off the pole plant will raise your upper body a bit, too. This makes you lighter so that you can steer the tips across the hill. At the advanced level you would normally begin to set what was your uphill ski immediately as you begin to unweight. For now, you can slide into the falline first before setting the new edge. You'll notice that with a wider stance you tend to stand on both skis along the foot area rather than transferring weight from tip to tail as you're able to do when the uphill ski is slid into the downhill ski.

You should also try this rebounding drill a number of times to either side . . . drop the hips, plant the pole, feel the edge set, lighten the body, and swing the skis across the falline with the tails of the ski on or off the snow. Again, do this a number of times to either side.

Beginning to Carve

Turning on one ski in practice can help break the habit of sliding or relying on two skis when weighting. To get the feel of driving your weight through the downhill ski edge, stand facing directly down the falline. (Normally, in a turn you would stay in the falline for just an instant. However, when trying to develop a new skill, like putting the ski on edge, you should give yourself some extra time. Instead of turning through the falline quickly, ski directly down the slope for an extra second or two with weight on both skis.) Let your skis slide down the hill; gradually pick the uphill ski off the snow as you take the knee of the downhill ski and drive it forward and up into the hill. Once the ski begins the turn, just apply even pressure as you stand in the middle of the ski. Repeat this turn in each direction until you feel balanced on one ski, then gradually place the uphill ski alongside the downhill ski, being careful to weight it just a little. You should be able to feel the inside edge of the downhill ski . . . a striking difference if you've been sliding on both ski edges.

Stepping

Once you are able to feel the way the ski reacts when you carve it halfway through the turn, you should try to work your way backwards, gradually setting the ski on edge at an earlier point in the turn. To do this, try stepping the uphill ski out into the falline laterally from a long radius turn as you rise from the anticipation position, and then put weight on it immediately. It will become the downhill ski. If you weight the ski, and turn the knees up into the hill, the ski will bite, instead of slide through a turn. This is a good exercise for skiers of all abilities.

Long Radius Turn

Long and Short Radius Turns

It's important to be able to feel the difference between long, medium, and short radius turns. Each type of turn requires a different edging quality, or angulation, and a somewhat different stance. To prepare for mogul skiing you should train on the flats making giant slalom, slalom, and short radius turns.

Long and medium radius turns, like those in GS, give you much more time to transfer your weight from one edge to another. You can do this by stepping laterally, almost up the hill, as mentioned earlier, which helps transfer weight onto the downhill ski, or you can keep both the skis parallel and on the snow. Regardless, anticipation occurs and the ski arches through, and accelerates out of the turn because the hips are dropped back slightly. This is an excellent turn to practice; it'll help you become comfortable accelerating out of a turn, as well as feel under control when your weight is back slightly.

For mogul skiing, ideally, you should not be on the tails of the ski. However, everyone ends up in this position at some time, either due to a sudden drop in the slope or a technical mistake. The point is to prepare yourself for all possible situations. If you feel your weight is in the rear and you've practiced this technique before, you'll know how to save the turn and pull out of trouble. Also, GS turns are a good way to practice skiing fast; there's nothing better for developing split second timing while having fun at the same time.

The slalom turn is shorter in radius than the GS turn, and it requires less time to set up. To oversimplify . . . slalom turns demand quick angulation from the knees down, while GS turns require greater angulation from the hips due to the speed of the turn. In slalom your weight is centered over the ski throughout most of the turn, rather than back slightly, as in GS. Other than this, the dynamics are the same, but everything

Short Radius Turn

just happens much more quickly in slalom turns. For this reason, it's essential that the body face squarely down the falline, and that the pole plant occur at the right time so that you initiate your turn early.

Each turn is dependent on the one before it; by skiing short radius turns, with or without a step, you can quickly find flaws in your technique. Mistakes pile up within a matter of turns, indicating whether you need to return to basics or go on. The short radius turn is very similar to a mogul turn, the main difference is that it doesn't require as much absorption. If you tried the rebounding drill and were able to swing the skis across the falline successfully, you were actually doing a short radius turn. Again, try to stand on the downhill ski.

Ski Stances

The lower the stance you take on skis, bending the knees and inclining them up into the hill, the more edge you place into the surface of the snow. To feel how high, medium, and low stances affect the ski, try the drills mentioned above in high, medium, and low body positions. A common error when trying to ski in a low stance is to bend at the waist. This places too much pressure forward and doesn't help you put the ski on edge in the least; that must be done with the knees as the upper body stays square.

You'll find that with a higher stance, the skis will take a bit longer to come around through the turn. A lower stance will tighten the radius of your turn. As you can imagine, in the moguls where short radius turns are needed, your body position is normally quite low in the middle of the turn; when you release the edges from the turn, your stance becomes higher as you extend the legs. After trying each of these body positions in the drills, try putting a complete turn together again, with the ski on edge, the body held relatively high. (Remember that a higher stance is correct for runs that are not very steep.)

Transferring from Edge to Edge

THE HOP TURN—The "hop turn" is a technique used when skiing extremely steep terrain. You transfer your weight directly from the downhill ski edge of one turn to the downhill ski edge of the next turn. The skis actually leave the snow between edge sets, and the sets help the skier control the speed of the descent by acting as a brake. It isn't a classic turn because you don't arch along the length of the ski edge. Rather, you transfer your weight directly from edge to edge. Practicing this hop turn on the flats helps you learn to keep the upper body facing down the falline squarely as the skis work back and forth across the hill. This drill reinforces the importance of the pole plant because it's impossible to do this without planting your poles to initiate the up-weighting. It also increases your awareness of how to use the ski edge to both accelerate and to slow down; it teaches you how to make your skis rebound into the next turn, and helps you develop rhythm.

Begin this drill by moving down the falline and dropping down hard into the anticipation position. Once the edges bite, pull the tails of your skis off the snow and swing them across the falline so that they face the opposite direction. When you do this, the tips of the skis remain pointing down the hill as the tails move back and forth like a pendulum.

should occur on the side of a mogul. After you have tried an edge jam to either side a number of times, try linking two and three of them together. Be sure to keep your skis on the snow at all times, set both edges simultaneously, hold the upper body square (facing down the falline), and make the pole plant strong.

INDEPENDENT LEG ACTION—Mogul skiing is different from alpine racing in the sense that slalom and GS emphasize independent leg action a great deal. In mogul skiing there is independent leg action too, but because of the tighter stance (legs closer together), the legs appear to work as a unit. Much less stepping is required in mogul skiing. The racer's stance is significantly wider than that of a mogul skier. Part of the reason for this is that race courses are set on smooth terrain. In a mogul field, if the skier retains a wide, stepping stance, the skis might rest on two different planes, or sides, of the mogul line. This makes it difficult to balance. If you rest the uphill ski in close to the downhill ski, it's easier to stay in the line, but as always, individual styles differ.

THE EDGE JAM—Next, try setting both edges hard, jamming them so that you stop abruptly. In this drill the point is to overexaggerate. Set the edge of the downhill ski while keeping the uphill ski light. When you've almost ended the turn, drop your hips quickly while inclining both knees sharply up into the hill. This is actually an edge jam, and it will stop you dead.

As unorthodox as this may sound, it is a good drill, for at times you will lose control and pick up too much speed in the moguls. When this happens, a quick jam can help you regain control. This strong edge set

EDGING ON ICE—Here is another exercise to practice before making the transition to the mogul field. This will also promote edge awareness. Try to find a spot on the trail which is icy and stand on it, knees inclined up the hill and edges "biting" into the snow. Slowly release the edges of the skis by rolling your knees downhill. As the skis begin to slide, roll the knees back into the hill. This will stop the side slip.

These drills will help you become more aware of your upper and lower body position, the edge of the ski, the transfer of weight, and eventually the feeling of the carve turn. Training on the flats is a terrific way to work on technique; it can save you hours of frustration in the moguls. Many skiers mistakenly believe that only beginners practice on flat terrain, but you should return to these slopes and drills as often as you can. These exercises can be a lot of fun, and you can always make up a few of your own, too.

Moguls on Increasingly Difficult Terrain

When you make the transition from flat slopes to gentle mogul terrain, you'll have to change your technique slightly by lowering your stance. It should look like this:

- Head centered between the shoulders, looking down the slope.
- Like the basic stance on flat terrain, the arms are bent slightly at the elbows and raised out and up.
- The hips face forward squarely, but are dropped a bit lower than on flat terrain.
- The feet are held closer than shoulder width apart.

Absorption and Extension

One of the main differences from a turn on the flats and one in the moguls is the method of absorption and extension. You recall that absorption is a bending of the knees while keeping the upper body square. In the moguls, anticipation with an edge set is actually absorption. The knees "suck" the mogul up like a spring, which enables the upper body to remain balanced. Absorption can occur at the apex of a mogul or in the trough. Absorption and extension enable you to contour the skis to changes in the surface of the snow. Extension occurs immediately after absorption, and is a retracting or uncoiling of the legs. After the knees bend to absorb a bump, the legs extend, giving the body a higher stance on the low side of the mogul.

To practice absorption and extension, try to traverse a mogul field by keeping your skis flush with the ground at all times. The knees must bend to accommodate the different angles of the moguls. You also must place the right amount of pressure on the tip and the tail of the ski. As you ski into the apex of the mogul, push your weight through the tips of the skis and let your knees rise. Once over the top, press the skis into the snow, letting the knees extend away from the body.

Probably the most troublesome part of skiing in moguls is staying in the line, in other words, making your turns the same length as the turns in the trough. To do this, you must be able to make short radius turns; that's why the drills on flat terrain are so impor-

tant. If you haven't quite mastered these short turns yet, you can train in the moguls by skiing them one at a time.

Beginning the Turn

So how do you start the first turn when standing at the top of a mogul field? You drop into it from above. As you traverse across the top of the mogul field, you'll ski

by different lines, or troughs. Pick one of these and prepare to slip down into it. First, cut across the top of the mogul in the basic intermediate stance. As you reach the top of a mogul, drop your hips, bend the knees in anticipation and absorption, and set the downhill ski edge by turning the knees up into the hill. As the edges catch and your motion is halted for an instant, plant the "downhill" pole.

After you've set the edge, let the ski tails swing in the opposite direction as you retract your knees and rebound away from the released edge, steering the ski tips into the trough between the moguls. Make sure to look down the falline in anticipation of the turn. When you've slipped into the line by extending the legs and are facing down the falline, begin to set the edge of the new downhill ski on the side of the mogul. Try to arch through the turn until you are facing in the opposite direction. Depending on ski conditions and the part of the mogul skied, the skis may leave the snow for an instant . . . no problem, as long as you feel the sensation of rebounding.

Ski one mogul at a time, to each side until you feel comfortable. Be careful to keep your upper body facing squarely downhill at the end of anticipation as you release the edge, otherwise you may point your hip through the turn instead of using the knees and ankles. When you feel as though you're carving halfway through the turn, try linking two, three, and four turns together. To link turns you must set your edge, or check, at the end of each turn; this, of course, is the anticipation stance for the next turn. The correct way to ski moguls is to stay in one line, skiing straight down the hill. But if you are new to this, it will be easier if you alternate between lines, simply because you'll acquire bad habits if you try to ski too far above your technical ability.

Setting the Edge Early

Once you're able to link turns together by setting the downhill ski on edge halfway through the turn, you should try setting the new edge from the beginning of the turn, as you are changing your weight, rebounding out of anticipation. This is a carve in the moguls. Practice stepping out of anticipation from one edge to the next. Take what is the uphill ski, and step laterally, placing it on the other side of the mogul line, so that the ski tip is pointing in the opposite direction. Place your weight completely on this new inside downhill ski edge, and pull the other ski in along side of it, arching through the turn. This is difficult, so don't expect to get it the first try!

After you've practiced stepping out of anticipation, try doing the same exercise but change the radius of your turns. Begin by making GS turns across the hill with a step and absorption, then gradually reduce the length of the turn to medium, and eventually short, radius steps back in the mogul line. It's very important that you absorb and extend in this drill to keep the skis on the snow.

Tight Turns in the Trough

A drill which can help you learn to stay in a tight trough is edge setting with a hop through the moguls. This is the same drill that you did on the flats, only you'll be hopping from edge to edge on uneven terrain. Ideally, you should try to stay on either side of the trough during this drill, but it's also good practice to edge set on all parts of the mogul. This will increase dexterity and prepare you for those moments when you misjudge a turn and find yourself on the wrong part of the mogul.

Choosing the Line

Before moving on to steeper mogul slopes, you should begin planning your turns in advance. In ski lingo, this is called "choosing a line." Though it sounds obvious, most skiers do not study mogul slopes, or plan where they're going to turn before pushing off. Learning to do this is a very good habit. Mentally, it helps you visualize what you're going to do. Physically, it teaches you to keep your head up while you're skiing, which improves your balance.

Skiing to Match the Quality of the Slope

As you progress onto steeper mogul terrain, you'll find that the quality of the slope changes a bit. On more advanced trails the moguls are larger, longer, closer together, and have less rhythm. Each of these factors requires a slight adjustment in technique. For now, though, let's imagine that you have before you the perfect mogul slope with an even pitch and nicely formed bumps!

Lowering of the Basic Stance

As you recall, the basic stance lowers as the steepness of the slope increases. To begin a series of turns on a steeper slope, stand above a line and decide where you're going to try to turn. Drop into it and set up in the anticipation position. In this terrain, the hips are dropped more during absorption, and the reach for the pole plant is slightly exaggerated. On a steeper slope, the body naturally picks up more speed. For this reason, the edge set during anticipation should be stronger to control your speed and give you more power to transfer, or rebound, your body into the next turn.

The rebound created from a strong edge set is the key to staying in a tight mogul line. If you've been turning in the moguls by alternating between two lines, in other words, skiing around the apex of the mogul because you can't stay in the line, it's time to progress. Practice the edge set jam mentioned earlier on flat terrain, then try to apply it on an advanced slope. If you've been trying to stay in the line, but can't because you pick up too much speed, try to build up the number of successive turns gradually.

Absorption and Extension on a Difficult Mogul Slope

As mentioned earlier, the quality of absorption and extension changes a bit as mogul terrain becomes more difficult. During anticipation you absorb as you set your edge, or you can absorb a bump on a flat ski. It depends upon which part of the mogul you're skiing over. Shallow terrain requires very little absorption, with more emphasis on a nice edge set. As the trail steepens you must "suck the bumps up" with your knees to keep the skis on the snow, and sometimes this means that the knees come up as high as the chest! It's quite common to find a "monster bump" in the middle of a perfect line! In this situation you have no choice but to absorb the mogul straight on, instead of carving along the side. It's done by driving the knees forward and letting them bend freely, instead of inclining them to one side.

This, of course, means that your extension must also be exaggerated after flat absorption. In extension, you should be trying to set the ski on edge. Think of "pressing" or "pushing" the skis along the mogul line as you incline the knees in the direction of your next turn. Again, think of absorption as "coiling up" and extension as "uncoiling" the legs as you set the edge.

Different Parts of the Mogul

It's a good exercise to ski different parts of the moguls at every stage: in the trough, on the side just above the trough, crest to crest with air in between, and from one line into the next. Each of these paths requires a change in the basic stance. A perfect run is very rare. If you train by skiing all possible angles of the mogul, you'll be prepared to handle diverse situations. Ultimately, this is what distinguishes a great skier from a good one.

Two main techniques are used for carving in a mogul line: one is to set the edge along the side of the mogul, just above the deepest part of the line; the other is to stay in the trough. When you think about it, the trough exists because the inside downhill ski edge is biting into the slope, pushing the snow to the side. Therefore, the path of least resistance would be to carve in the "belly" of the trough. There are many styles of mogul skiing though; that is the beauty of the sport. One thing is certain, turning is easier if you hold a tight stance, with legs somewhat close together and the feet working as a unit. The inside edges of both skis may appear to be set at the same time, but actually most of the pressure is on the downhill ski, and the uphill ski rests alongside, aiding in stability.

Skiing crest to crest requires that you intentionally ski from the top of one mogul to the top of the next. To do this you have to steer your skis toward the apex of the mogul. When you are at the crest you pop very slightly, straightening the body. This will lift you into the air. Try to land just before the crest of the next mogul, pushing away, or extending the legs just after you touch down. This will keep your upper body from collapsing. To change lines, steer across the crest of the mogul instead of straight into it, and pop harder to gain more distance.

Once you've readjusted to skiing in the line again, try changing your stance. Intentionally ski with your hips dropped back, with them pushed forward, and with them inclined up into the hill. Concentrate on how these incorrect stances feel, and experiment with techniques that will help you regain your balance over the middle of the ski. If you're too far back, force your

Different Parts of the Mogul

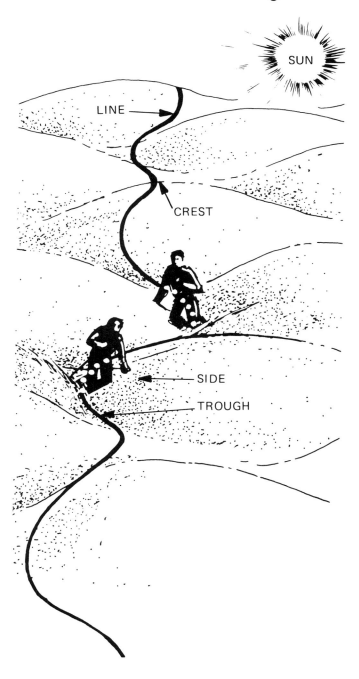

hands forward; if you're too far forward, lift your head and shoulders up; if you're inclining your hips into the hill, strengthen and reach for your pole plant to help you initiate anticipation correctly. By forcing mistakes in a controlled setting, you can practice recovering. Eventually, you'll be able to react within hundredths of a second.

Increase the Number of Turns

At this point, it is important to begin increasing the number of successive turns. Standing at the top of a run, look down the slope and choose a line. As you ski, try to count the number of turns you're able to make in a row. Counting increases your awareness of rhythm and makes you look ahead for the next turn. Gradually you should be able to ski longer pitches, and eventually whole parts of a run.

Again, if you're having trouble controlling your speed, review the abrupt braking drill on the flats. Practice hop turns, and then hard edge sets in the moguls. When you return to skiing a complete pitch, pick up speed intentionally, then throw in a hard edge set to help get your feet back underneath your hips.

Typical Balance Problems

Some typical problems encountered at this stage may cause you to lose your balance. See if you recognize some of these, and try to correct them before moving on to a steeper mogul slope. Otherwise, you may simply compound the problem.

Leaning Back

Turns are initiated on the front of the ski. However, when a skier leans back the turn is erroneously initiated right around the boot area, and pressure on the ski is concentrated on the tails. It's difficult to turn the ski this way. On bumpy terrain, before long you will lose your balance to the rear because the hips are behind, instead of over the middle of, the ski. To force the body forward and to bring the hips back to the center, push your arms in front of you and reach for the pole plant.

Make sure that you're absorbing the bump instead of "pushing off" of it, and let your knees retract toward the chest.

Leaning Forward

At the other extreme, leaning too far forward can also get you into some pretty crazy ski positions. Most skiers find themselves falling over their tips because

they've bent at the waist too much. This typically occurs during absorption on a flat ski. It can also happen if the tips of the skis get caught on the apex of a mogul, stopping you abruptly. To get out of trouble, try lifting your head and pushing your shoulders up, as you simultaneously drop your hips slightly to the rear. These things ought to take some of the pressure off the tips of your skis, and right your upper body.

Arm Caught Behind

Another problem at this stage is holding the arms out too far to the side. If you do this, either arm can get caught behind you. Depending on how you compensate for the mistake, you can lose your balance forward or to the rear. Make sure you reach out in front for the pole plant, and that you begin your turn on the tip of the ski rather than at the foot area.

Movement of the Upper Body

Body movement during a turn occurs mainly from the waist down, with the exception of the hands reaching forward for the pole plant. The upper torso should remain quiet. If the knees and ankles are not working back and forth across the falline, the skier must compensate to somehow create the force needed to turn the skis. The most common mistake is swinging the upper body through the turn by pointing a shoulder blade, hip, or hand in the direction of the desired turn. To correct this, return to the flats and practice short radius turns. Concentrate on driving your knee through the turn and on keeping your body square. If you're still moving the upper body, hold both poles in front of you with the baskets in the left hand and the grips in the right. This should square the shoulders, making you turn with the lower body.

Incorrect Turning Radius

One of the most important elements of skiing moguls is to contour the skis and the body to the change in slope. This means that the length of your turns should be the same length as the change in the mogul line. Many skiers try to ski down a mogul slope by making turns that are different in length than the terrain demands. You can spot this problem easily; the skier looks as though he's fighting his way down the hill, muscling the skis through each turn. To correct the habit, go back to the basics of short-swing on the flats. Running some slalom gates is a good idea, too.

Fine Tuning Your Mogul Technique on Tough Terrain

If your basic stance has progressively closed, and you're able to drop into a mogul line, anticipate, lower your hips and set your edge with knees inclined up into the hill, plant the pole, unweight, and extend smoothly as you carve along the side of the mogul line . . . if orchestration is complete . . . then what?

You can play a number of drills and games to improve your balance, timing, speed, and technique. These types of drills are important; they can prevent you from reinforcing old bad habits, and they can force you to challenge yourself. It's easy to become comfortable with your own ski style, but this is a mistake. You can always improve!

A Change of Pace

Changing pace within your run is a good drill to practice. This is one of the signs of a skier who is in complete control of a slope, regardless of pitch or size of the moguls. You need to be able to "let your skis go" as well as "put the brakes on." Changing speed can save you from a dangerous situation like hitting a rock or skiing into someone's way. In mogul competition, where part of the judging criteria relies on speed, you must be able to accelerate at will, while remaining smooth and in control. You can practice this drill in a

couple of ways: by beginning slowly and increasing speed gradually, by exploding into the first turn as you would out of the starting gate, or by changing pace within the run. To accelerate, make your edge sets a little weaker and cut your turn a bit short by not letting your skis turn across the falline as much.

Speed control is a great asset if you're planning on skiing in mogul competition dual format (see Chapter 9). Being out in front has its advantages in dual competition; you're less distracted by the other skier, and the judge's eyes tend to focus on the skier who's in the lead. Being able to slow your speed down comes in handy when you're preparing to jump in the moguls, or when you're on the verge of falling. If you can control your speed, you'll be ready to deal with surprises.

Improving Upper Body Control

Skiing without poles can help improve upper body control and overall balance. As you ski down the slope,

cise on the flats, and gradually make the transition to bumpy terrain. Most skiers are stronger turning in one direction than the other, so be prepared to have some trouble at first. When turning on the weak side, you put more pressure on the pole that you are planting. This will lighten the load on the ski edge, making it easier to turn. You will quickly notice that when the leg with the ski on it is the downhill leg, you can carve a turn as you normally would. But, when it becomes the uphill leg you must tip the ski onto its outside edge by turning the knee out, instead of in, and by leaning slightly into the hill. To ski on one leg in the moguls, your anticipation and edge set are the same as on two skis. However, to release the edge you might need to lift the tail of the ski off the snow at first. Obviously, your hips, knees, and feet must be underneath you or you will quickly lose your balance.

hold your arms out in front, as if you had imaginary poles in your hands. Sink into anticipation, make a quick, downward motion with the downhill arm, as you would if you had a pole. The rebound, which is so important in mogul skiing, must come from the edge set and unweighting, without the help of the poles as a third balance point. The leg muscles must pull the skis out of the edge set as the upper body remains square and quiet. You can feel the extra load as the quadriceps and hamstrings begin to burn . . . great for training! It's especially important to keep your skis on the snow at all times in this drill. Think of "pressing" the skis against the surface of the snow. You must really have a handle on absorption and extension, and this drill lets you find out how these skills are coming along.

Balance and Edge Training on One Leg

Skiing on one ski is great for developing balance and increasing edge awareness. It's best to begin this exer-

Training with Dual Format

Skiing side by side in dual format is a lot of fun, and it's very good training as well. Skiing hard against someone who is right next to you is completely different from skiing at your own pace. It gives you an immediate frame of reference. With the skier beside you, you can tell if you're skiing slower, if you need to jump, if you've got to increase the number of turns, or if you are easily distracted. And as always, by training in a competitive situation, you tend to push yourself harder.

Cat and Mouse

Once you've become confident in the moguls, it's easy to fall into a routine of skiing the same way every run. Not only is this bad for your technique, but it leads to boredom. You should continue to take chances, if you want to progress. A good drill to fit into a day of skiing is "cat and mouse." Try to follow someone else's line through the moguls; you'll be surprised how difficult this is, and how tough it is to change your style to fit that of another person.

Finding Optimum Speed

Another good drill is trying to find your optimum speed on a particular slope. To pick up speed intentionally, reduce the pressure of your edge sets and the angle of deflection of the skis across the falline, and try to flatten the skis a bit more so that the base comes in contact with the snow more often. Also, if you place your hips back a little, you can accelerate out of the turn, thus picking up speed. Time yourself with a stop watch, or simply try to ski to a point where you're on the verge of falling. In fact, if you're competing, you should certainly fall on the course before your competition run. If you find that you're sacrificing speed for form, slow down a bit, but let your skis run. Let yourself ride that fine line between control and disaster! By knowing what your optimum speed is on a slope, you can ski just below that level. But there's no way to find that point unless you go beyond it, and often that means falling.

Saving an Incorrect Turn

If you're skiing the moguls and suddenly lose control, you may be able to use one of several techniques to save the turn. One of them is the double pole plant. Keep in mind that this is not a good habit, but it can help pull you out of trouble. As mentioned earlier, the pole plant is actually a third balance point. Not only does it help you initiate a turn by making unweighting possible, but it keeps your hands forward. Many times balance is lost to the rear because the non-pole planting hand drops behind. If you force this hand forward, and create a fourth balance point by planting it quickly in the snow, you can regain control. Use this technique only if you must; it's not handsome, and it usually signifies recovery from a mistake.

Increasing Distance

At the same time that you increase your speed in the moguls, you should try increasing the distance that you ski at one time. Try to ski complete pitches, stay in the falline, and ski in a straight line from one point to another. Having mastered this, ski nonstop from the top of a mogul trail to the bottom, and eventually from the top of the mountain to the bottom. This will tax you cardiovascularly, as well as give you a leg burn.

Jumping in the Bumps

Jumping in the moguls is exhilarating and always a challenge. It's the most spontaneous part of mogul skiing, certainly the most fun, and definitely the most difficult! You should know a few things about jumping before you go off to try it on your own.

If you're just learning to jump, it's very helpful to choose a mogul ahead of time which has a good "shelf" to lift off and a good landing. Look for the top of a mogul that is somewhat flat, one that slopes out instead of up. If it's flat on top, you'll have more time to prepare for the pop, and the angle will throw you out and up, rather than back and up. A mogul that is "scooped" out is one to stay clear of at first; this can put your hips back even before you've popped off the

lip of the mogul. After you know which mogul you're going to jump off, try to pick a spot to land. Again, look for the shelf of a mogul, or better yet, try to land on the side of the mogul which slopes into the trough or line. If you can land here, it's very easy to put the ski on edge immediately without breaking rhythm. But landing on the flat top of a mogul is fine, too; it will just take a little longer to carve into the next turn.

The first time you jump from a mogul, you should just ride off holding the basic stance position. (After you've become comfortable with this, and you're able to land without problem, then you should try a maneuver.) With the take off and the landing planned, ski toward the mogul. As you reach the shelf, flatten both of the skis, make sure both of your hands are in front of you, and bend the knees. When you reach the lip of the mogul, extend the body just a little. Once in the air, hold your body in a low stance.

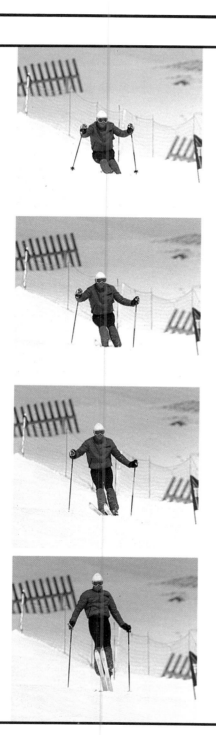

After you feel comfortable doing this, gradually add more of a pop by straightening the knees and quickly lifting the arms up in front of you. You'll be balanced because your body will be on axis when it is extended. The head, hips, and feet will form a straight line.

The landing is the trickiest part of jumping in the moguls. It's easy to take off, and once in the air there are no obstacles, but—oh—to land! The landing depends on the pop to some extent. To land in the spot that you've chosen, you've got to be able to feel how strongly you should extend during the pop. This can only come with practice. Assuming the pop is correct, you should be prepared to absorb the impact of dropping to the ground by relaxing the legs. This will make it easy for them to bend as you touch down, absorbing the landing with the knees. After the initial bend in the

knees, you should try to straighten them, as if "punching" or "pushing" away from the mogul immediately after you touch down. Don't let the mogul make contact with your skis; you make contact with the mogul. It sounds confusing, but think of it as pushing away from the mogul as you land. This will keep your upper body from collapsing on itself. Practice putting your ski on edge immediately after you land. Eventually, you'll be able to land in a carve turn, with the edge of the skis angled into the snow.

A number of different maneuvers can be performed once in the air, such as a spread eagle, twister, or zudnic-spread. The specifics of each of these jumps are reviewed in the aerial chapter subtitled: "Individual Maneuvers in the Air," found on page 86. Look this over and if you have a chance, try the maneuver standing on the ground, just to get the feel of it.

There are a host of other drills you can do to keep pushing yourself both in the moguls and in your ski technique in general. It could be a book in itself! Try the drills in this chapter, then try to think up some of your own. Get other people involved. If you're at all competitive, you'll push yourself like never before. And don't make the mistake of thinking that to be an expert mogul skier, you should just ski moguls . . . . If you did this, you most certainly would lose the joy of it, and it would be evident in both your mood and your technique. Ski the flats, ski fast, slow, long, short, jump a little, run some gates, take a ski off, chase someone, ski the woods, the powder, teach a friend, ski the crud . . . . These are the things that will make you a dynamic mogul skier. And they will most certainly change your attitude about almost any skiing activity.

CHAPTER 3

Ballet

At the World Cup level, ballet skiing is extremely specialized. Yet it is a facet of skiing which can be enjoyed by people of all ages, by anyone seeking the challenge and variety of training the body to move with grace and power. You can use ballet maneuvers to complement overall body awareness and to increase edge control, or you can dive right in with the intention of competing. Regardless of your ultimate intentions, ski ballet can improve your sense of balance, coordination, flexibility, and timing. This is not a new idea. It's not uncommon today to find football players in dry land dance classes plieing and reveleing across the floor in their sweats, or world class alpine racers practicing ski ballet on 150 cm skis on the Austrian glaciers during the summer.

It makes sense. Ballet skiing, like dance and ice skating, requires remarkable body control. These athletes understand, to a science, the dynamics of body line, form, and choreography—foot part touching snow, floor, ice. Through the media of music and body movement, the ballet skier can evoke emotion in the hearts of spectators. What a supreme gift, what greater power than to momentarily erase people's cares, draw them into music, and interpret it using your body as the instrument!

As a competitor, attaining complete control is an ideal, but not always a realistic goal. It's true that the ballet event is much more predictable than, say, the mogul event; routines are choreographed and tricks are mapped out along the course. Despite this deliberateness, outside factors can affect your performance. For instance, visibility, snow conditions, running order, minor injuries, and the subjective values of the judges all may influence your score.

> The power of will
> is measured not only
> by intense desire, but
> as much by composure
> and an almost selfless
> precision and lightness.
>
> DICK TAYLOR

But some things you can control, such as the degree to which you perfect the basic maneuvers of ballet skiing. This is important because it will determine whether you're able to progress to more difficult stunts. If you can do a 360 degree rotation in the air from a strong edge set, with the body "on axis," the 540, 720, and 900 degree rotations can be learned progressively. However, technique problems manifest themselves in various forms as you try to increase the difficulty of your tricks.

How long will it take you to learn these moves? Individuals progress at different rates; it really depends

on the time invested in training, individual levels of athleticism, attitude, and coaching staff, to mention a few factors! But it's safe to say that with the correct equipment and the right attitude the basic maneuvers can be learned quite quickly.

Try some of these ballet moves both on and off the snow. Have fun with the beginning maneuvers: the linking steps, called illusions and leg breakers; 360 degree spins and jumps; and front and back pole flips. You may just discover that you have a natural aptitude for this. In addition, the skills you may develop—spotting, body axis, line, form, rotation, and overall body awareness in the air—will help your balance in other ski events such as mogul skiing, jumping, and alpine racing.

I. Linking Steps

Illusions and leg breakers are used to link different tricks together. They help the skier make the most of what would otherwise become "empty space" in the routine. In fact, by combining linking maneuvers with choreography, the ballet skier can create a performance with mood and emotion that may well surpass the degree of difficulty of the tricks themselves. Jan Bucher, seven-time world ballet champion, beautifully balances degree of difficulty with emotion. Her routines are electrically charged with dangerous spins, jumps, and pole flips, yet she executes them without sacrificing line or form. You remember Jan's performances. She communicates a beauty of motion, a harmony between body and music so complete, that sometimes a person is pressed to remember whether Jan actually had skis on her feet at all.

Linking steps should not be an albatross around the ballet skier's neck. Rather, they should give the skier an opportunity to express himself and to define his specific style. It's easy to pick out a skier who is simply "going through the motions" of getting from one trick to another. You have to take a chance, become totally involved in what you're trying to express, and make your performance as memorable as possible.

The Illusion

An illusion is one of the linking steps that you can use to create mood within a piece, or to make use of the hill. It begins from a basic crossover, or javelin, position. Pick the downhill ski up off the snow and cross it over the front of the uphill ski, transferring weight to the uphill ski. To initiate an uphill spin, apply pressure to the ball of the foot and simultaneously pivot as you steer the uphill ski into the hill. The elevated leg which was crossed over the uphill ski should then be un-crossed as you pivot, and turned 360 degrees. The ski on the snow should continue to spin to 180 degrees as the weight is released from it, and transferred to the uncrossed ski as the ski is placed on the snow in the opposite direction.

The illusion will work smoothly if you continue to spin. If you stop spinning, the effect of the illusion will be destroyed and the maneuver will look like a simple "uncross."

The Leg-Breaker

In the illusion you begin with your skis crossed and finish with them uncrossed. In the leg-breaker you begin with the skis parallel, cross them, and finish with them crossed or uncrossed! Sound confusing? Start in the basic traverse position and initiate an uphill spin by skating up the hill on the outside edge of the uphill ski. As you apply pressure and the uphill ski begins to spin, lift the downhill ski and let it pivot in the air, placing the tip in and behind the tail of the spinning ski. After the ski is tucked in behind, transfer your weight onto it. You can then step out of this position at 180 degrees, resuming the traverse position, or you can continue spinning to 360 degrees with your skis crossed.

II. Spins

The Two-Footed 360 Degree Spin

The two-footed 360 degree spin is one of the maneuvers you must master before moving on to more difficult tricks. You'll use parts of this spin in practically everything else you learn in ballet. Begin the 360 degree spin by traveling either across or down the falline with weight placed equally on both skis. Initiate the spin by making a parallel turn up into the hill, transferring your weight onto the balls of your feet. Reaching 180 degrees through the spin (facing uphill) you should be on flat skis, leaning forward slightly. Spinning the last half of the rotation, your weight will naturally shift back a little and on to the new downhill ski. Gravity will pull your skis back into the falline.

Keep the upper body straight and high and look in the direction of the spin.

The One-Footed 360 Degree Spin

One-footed spins are maneuvers which will eventually lead you into jumps like the tip drag 360 and the inside axel, so learn them well. While traveling across the hill with your legs about shoulder width apart, slowly transfer your weight onto the uphill ski by bending the knee of the uphill leg and driving it forward. At the same time let the downhill leg lag behind a bit and then push off it as if it were skating onto the uphill ski. Pushing off the downhill leg will help you initiate the spin by driving your weight forward, which pushes the uphill ski into the turn. This also gives you the momentum to raise the downhill leg behind the body. As the downhill ski is raised behind the head the arms should open out to the sides for balance. When you begin to spin up the hill, the pressure is on the outside of the uphill ski. When you are halfway around it is transferred to the bottom of the foot, making the ski lie flat. Through the last half of the rotation pressure control is concentrated on the inside of the ski. Always lead in the direction of the rotation with the head, and be conscious of line and form created by the arms and legs.

The Javelin Spin

A javelin is actually a one-footed 360 with the uphill ski crossed over in front of the downhill ski. It's a move which can lead you into a host of tricks like the camel spin or the sit spin. While traversing the slope, pick the uphill ski off the snow and cross it over the downhill ski. Hold the upper body high and the arms out to the side for balance. To initiate the spin, place pressure on the inside edge of the downhill ski as you would in a normal turn. Steer the ski up into the hill by putting extra pressure on the front of the ski, while leaning slightly forward. As the ski continues to spin just past 180 degrees, you will be gliding backwards on the tail of the ski. To keep turning, your weight will naturally shift forward a little to keep the tail from digging into the snow, as well as to the outside of the foot which is spinning. To step out, push the raised ski forward and step out onto the snow, and transfer your weight on to this ski immediately, assuming the traverse position. Remember: always keep the head, shoulders, and hips turning in the direction of the rotation.

The Sit Spin (variation on a javelin)

To initiate a sit spin you will need to increase momentum within the spin to compensate for the open leg position, because the more open the body the slower the rotation. By swinging the arms away from the direction of spin (counter-rotating) and then suddenly throwing them into the spin, you can produce more spinning power. From your traverse, swing both arms away from the direction of the spin. When they become blocked by the upper body and hips, quickly change direction, throwing them back around and up into the hill. The momentum created by this arm movement will turn the skis up into the hill, carving on the inside edge of the downhill ski. Complete a full revolution as you would for an inside 360. As you begin your second revolution, take the uphill ski and cross it over the downhill ski in the javelin position. Drop your hips and bend at the waist. Hold this position as you spin, leading with the head and the uphill arm. To come out of the spin, begin lifting the crossed ski up and out of the javelin position as you straighten your body. You'll do this about three-quarters of the way through the spin, then raise the uphill ski in front of you and you're back in an inside spin.

Tip-Tails

You can perform a tip-tail spin as you step out of the leg-breaker position, one ski pointing up the hill, the other pointing down. With each leg bent comfortably at the knee, push off the back leg, placing all your weight on the outside edge of the uphill ski. Raise the downhill ski in back of you and as you spin up into the hill, pull it around in front of your body. When you reach 180 degrees into the spin (and are facing up the hill) the tip of what was the uphill ski should be pressing into the hill. At the same time, the tail of the ski which was raised should be placed on the snow next to the tip of the other ski. If you flex your quadriceps and press up onto the tip and tail of the skis, you can spin by leading with the head, shoulders, and hips. Notice how the arms are held out to the side for balance and the back is arched to create an attractive line. You can stop spinning by releasing the press from the downhill ski, letting the tail slip back down onto the snow. This will in turn release pressure from the tip of the other ski, and you can return to a regular two-foot spin.

The Camel Spin (variation on an inside spin)

The camel spin has been adopted from figure skating
and is one of the most beautiful one-footed spins. In a
camel, the leg which is raised up and behind creates a
straight line with the torso and head, which are tipped
forward, perpendicular to the downhill leg. You initiate
this spin somewhat differently than other spins. In preparation for spinning up the hill, brake into a shallow
snowplow, bending slightly at the waist. Steer the
downhill ski across the falline and straighten the downhill leg as you lift the uphill leg, pushing off the snow.
Gradually bring the uphill leg from in front of your
body to behind, keeping the leg straight. You'll need to
keep your weight on the tails of the ski to balance while
holding the uphill ski in front. As you place the leg
behind you, your weight should shift on to the tips of
the ski. This happens quite naturally as the upper torso
dips down toward the snow. The uphill leg, which is
lifted above and behind the head, creates a straight line
with the torso. To enhance form, push the chest out
and arch the back, keeping the arms out to the side
for balance. To step out of this maneuver drop the
back leg slowly, straightening the upper body at the
same time.

III. Jumps

Each of the jumps, or rotations in the air, as they are most commonly called, begin from one basic position: the edge set. The key to performing jumps correctly is to take the forward momentum gained from skiing either down or across the falline, and transfer it straight up. To do this you must first "stop" forward momentum by setting the edge of the ski hard, and then lifting your body up off the balls of your feet. This edge set is often referred to as a "J-stroke" because of the hook-like imprint it leaves in the snow. It is the most rudimentary part of all jumping maneuvers, whether you're performing a simple 360 or a 900 degree rotation.

Setting up for a jump can be done a number of ways. An edge set can begin anywhere from a shallow traverse to straight down the falline.

While it's possible to come into a jump from a number of angles (from straight on or arching into it), the J-stroke and the edge set should be performed the same way each time. With the exception of small, individual variations, the edge set should occur just past the point where your skis are perpendicular to the line of travel. Most mistakes in jumps happen because the skier misses, or makes a poor edge set. Instead of power being transferred up, it is mistakenly transferred forward. In this case, distance is gained as the skier "travels," while height is lost. The result is often an inability to complete the full rotation or the body rotating "off axis."

If the J-stroke and the edge set are learned correctly from the start, single maneuvers can easily develop into doubles, and variations of these jumps can be learned safely. The J-stroke is a simple traverse with a "loop" or uphill turn on the end. The position of the traverse depends, of course, on the maneuver. For simplicity's sake let's use a 360. Traverse the hill in a high basic stance with feet about shoulder width apart and weight equally on both skis. To initiate the "loop," put pressure on the downhill ski as you would for a normal turn and steer your skis up "into" the hill. The edge set is almost an edge jam. It's a dynamic, abrupt motion that occurs at the same time as the pole plant. In setting an edge, you must drop your weight down and incline your knees into the hill. This will put the skis on edge. The harder you set, the quicker you will stop the forward momentum. If you lift your body weight up immediately after the edge set by pushing off the poles and straightening the knees and torso at the same time, you can clear the ground and begin to rotate.

The Tip Drag 360

To begin the tip drag 360, make a shallow traverse across the hill, then take the uphill ski and let the tip of it catch in the snow by straightening the leg and pointing the foot down. The drag created by the ski tip's trailing in the snow will start to spin you around backwards. As you reach the end of the J-stroke, plant the poles as you set the inside edge of the downhill ski, inclining the knee into the hill, transferring your weight straight up by pushing off the poles, and straightening the knees and upper body. To help the body leave the snow, take the uphill ski which was dragging and kick it up high behind the back. Once in the air, turn the kicking leg out in the direction of the jump, pulling the hips through. As the edge-setting leg straightens and the downhill ski leaves the ground, the body will auto-matically begin to spin. Once the edge-setting ski leaves the ground, tension is released and the body will snap in the direction of the rotation, like a wound-up rubberband as it's released. Make sure that your head and hips are leading the tip drag around. If you're having trouble making it all the way around, practice doing a 180 first until you're comfortable.

Increasing the rotation from a 360, to 540, and eventually 720, is accomplished by bringing the arms in closer to the body and increasing the speed of the approach. The edge set and take-off are the same. Beginners sometimes mistakenly try to start the tip drag 360 directly off the ground. Wait until your body is in the air before beginning your rotation.

Inside Axel 360

An inside axel is so called because one ski is planted "inside," or crossed over and planted "above," the other ski. It requires the same approach as an illusion. From a shallow or steep approach, lift the downhill ski up and cross it over the uphill ski. The crossed leg is the edge-setting leg in this maneuver. Carve what was the uphill ski into a turn. When the turn has come around just before the falline, set the edge with the ski that has been crossed over in front. As you set the edge, plant the poles in close to the body on either side of the skis. As the momentum of the traverse is stopped by the edge set, transfer your weight upward by pushing up from the poles while straightening the body. You'll be able to increase the lift of the jump by straightening the new downhill ski leg and driving your heel up in back of you. The body should rise easily off the ground. Once in the air, turn in the direction of the rotation with the head, shoulders, and hips. Matching both legs by squeezing them together will increase the speed of your rotation and keep your body on axis.

Remember to keep your head up when you set your edge in this jump. Likewise, do not bend your upper body when you plant your poles; you'll lose power this way, not to mention form. Lastly, push up from your pole plant, not out.

Two-Footed Tip Vault

Traversing in the standard position with the skis shoulder width apart, begin the edge set with the J-stroke. Bend the knees and set both edges quickly by dropping your hips and turning your knees into the hill. At the same time, plant your poles uphill of the skis and rock onto the tips, pushing up from the poles with the arms. Straighten the body as it rises so that it will remain on axis. There's a point at the top of your tip vault where the tips of the skis will bend and then "uncoil," rebounding you into the direction of the rotation. Again, turn the head, shoulders, and hips in the direction of the rotation. If you try to lead with the feet in this maneuver the upper body may counter the motion, and the rotation will be blocked by the hips instead of led by them.

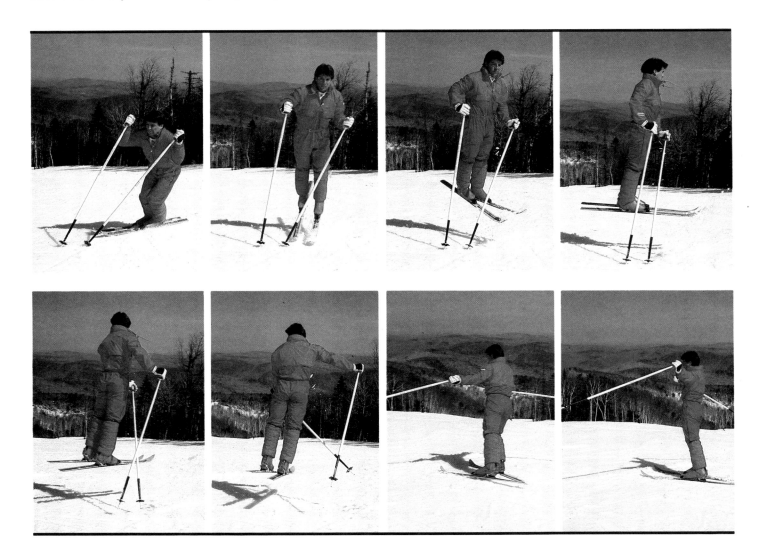

Stay Cross Axel

The edge set in the stay cross axel is the same as in the inside axel, but from a crossover position. Instead of crossing the downhill ski over in front of the uphill ski and then uncrossing the uphill ski in the middle of the rotation, leave it crossed. The rotation is still led with the head, shoulders, and hips. To aid in spinning, pull the foot of the crossed ski in tight to the other foot and press the hips forward. The rotation in a stay cross will be slower than an inside axel because the crossed position is more open. You can compensate for this by squeezing the legs and feet together as close as possible. When you land, it should be on the uphill ski, in the center of the foot area. Remember to keep your weight on the edge-setting leg at all times; if you transfer the weight to the back leg you're liable to fall.

Thumper

In a 360 degree thumper you edge set as in the tip drag, kicking your back leg as high as possible, at the same time as you push off your poles. As you start to rotate, cross your edge-setting leg over the kicking leg and squeeze your feet together to complete one rotation.

A 720 and a 900 thumper have the same edge set but less of a leg kick because they have a tendency to throw you off axis. Instead of kicking high, kick moderately. By squeezing your feet sooner you'll rotate faster. Also, the more speed you're able to generate going into the edge set, the more power you can transfer into the spin.

IV. Pole Flips

Split Pole Flip

The split pole flip is the most basic of flips. It's easiest because the body is allowed to drop down between the poles, requiring less height and arm strength. To begin, grasp your poles so that the palms of your hands are resting over the top of the pole grips.

Facing downhill, plant the poles in the snow so that they are slightly wider than shoulder width apart. (They should be at about a 70 degree angle to your body before initiating the flip.) To initiate the flip, bring the right foot up in front of you. As you pull the leg back down, let your upper body drop between the poles with the head leading. You should consciously look for the baskets and then watch them as you go upside down. When the right foot has been brought back down to the snow, kick the left leg back and straight over your head. Between 12 and 1 o'clock the feet and the legs should match. Still watching the baskets, pull up with the arms at one o'clock. Tuck the chin into the chest and look for the landing. You must touch down with bent knees to absorb the landing, but straighten as soon as possible.

To add a half twist you should initiate the trick in the same way as the simple split. When you are perpendicular to the ground, instead of looking at the baskets of the poles, look about two feet in front of them. Glue your eyes to this spot throughout the maneuver. Initiate the twist by turning the shoulders and hips in the direction you wish to spin, and continue to push away from the poles with your arms. This should turn you 180 degrees in the air, so that you're facing uphill when you land.

To complete a full twist, begin as you would a half twist. At one o'clock, the shoulders and hips should continue to rotate. The head should turn with the shoulders and hips, instead of spotting in front of the pole baskets. The poles, which were split at this point in the half twist, are brought together as you push hard away from the pole plant. This push with the arms will help you spin. When you complete this maneuver, you should be facing down the hill.

The Gut Pole Flip

In a gut pole flip you begin with your hands together instead of apart. (You should actually feel your knuckles rubbing together.) Hold your poles at about belly button height, slightly in front of your body. With the hands and poles held ready, let the skis slide directly down the falline. To initiate the flip and gain momentum, kick one of your legs up in front of you and rock back with your upper body. Bring the leg back down to the snow. While doing this, plant the poles and simultaneously kick the opposite leg up and in back as you bend at the waist. This should transfer your weight onto your poles. By pushing "away" from the ground with your arms and matching your legs together at 12 o'clock, you will begin to flip. Keep your eyes on the baskets. As the body is laid out at about one o'clock, push hard with the arms and tuck the chin into the chest. When you feel yourself dropping, look for the landing.

Gut Pole Flip with a Half Twist

Initiating a gut pole flip with a half twist is identical to initiating a simple gut. The half twist is added when the poles and the body are almost perpendicular to the slope. At this point, push off the poles and turn the shoulders in the direction that you wish to twist. Instead of tucking the chin into the chest, keep your eyes on the baskets of your poles.

Gut Pole Flip with a Full Twist

A gut pole flip with a full twist begins in the same manner as a simple gut. The full twist in this maneuver must begin at about nine o'clock as you are pushing your body up, even before your legs have matched. Begin turning your shoulders in the direction of the twist at about nine o'clock. As your body reaches 12 o'clock the legs should be brought together while you continue to twist. A "closed" position will increase the speed of the rotation, enabling you to finish the twist before you touch the snow. Up until this point you should be spotting the baskets of your poles. At one o'clock you should gradually begin to turn your head away from your poles and in the direction of the falline, making sure to push "away" from your poles at the same time. This will both continue the twist and give you enough clearance to drop cleanly onto the slope, facing straight down the falline.

The Rock and Roll

The beginning of a rock and roll is similar to a gut pole flip. The grips of the poles are held close together with the knuckles rubbing, but the base of the poles are spread apart slightly wider than shoulder width. The "rock" begins by letting the skis slide down the falline and planting the poles. With the arms and elbows straight, make your upper body stiff and let the front of your skis slide in between your poles. As the front of your ski boots pass an imaginary line between the poles, lift yourself into the air by pushing up with your arms, keeping the pole grips together against your lower abdomen. "Rock" forward slowly, letting the skis swing through until the poles are perpendicular to the slope. (You may have to break a little at the waist to keep your balance.) When the poles are resting at 12 o'clock break forward at the waist to initiate the "roll." Looking down at your poles, force the heels of both feet up over your head until your body is laid out at 12 o'clock, parallel with the ski poles. To complete the second half of the flip push your body "away" from your poles with a strong arm thrust, and remain laid out by trying to reach for the ground with your toes. You'll drop slowly onto the snow.

Rock and Roll with a Half Twist

Follow the same steps as a simple rock and roll until your body is completely laid out at 12 o'clock, perpendicular to the slope. At this point, while looking at the baskets of your poles, begin to turn your shoulders in the direction you wish to twist. Keep pushing away from your poles until you complete a half revolution and gravity will aid you in dropping onto the slope.

Rock and Roll with a Full Twist

Again, follow the beginning steps of the basic rock and roll, but make the swing from the pole plant to 12 o'clock stronger. This will enable you to extend your body out farther, making the twisting faster. The important thing to remember is to begin twisting when the body is perpendicular to the slope, as in the half twist. Once you've completed the half twist, keep turning your head and shoulders another half revolution as if looking up first toward the sky, continuing the look until your body has been brought back into the falline, falling naturally onto the snow.

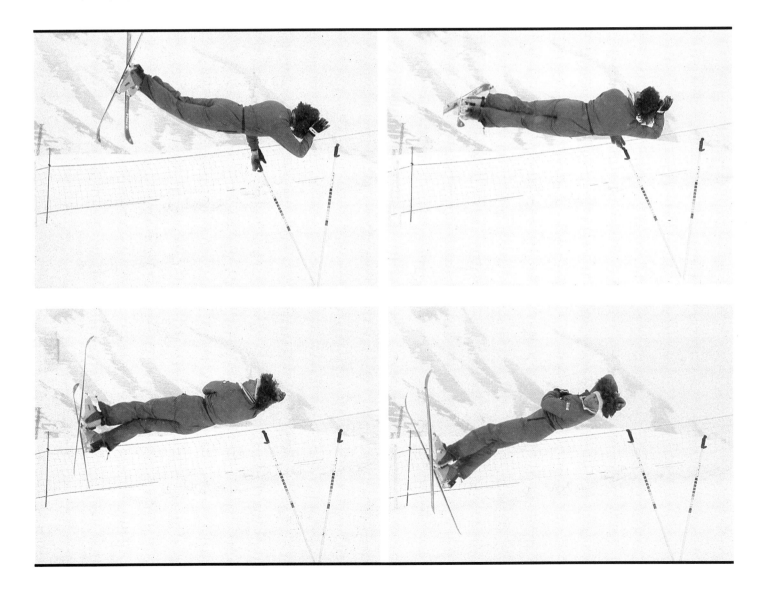

Back Pole Flip

To perform a back pole flip most ballet skiers begin by facing up the hill. This makes the maneuver a little easier because the slope of the hill falls away from you, giving you a few extra degrees to complete the trick.

In this maneuver the pole grip is different than in a split or gut flip. The palms of the hands face the torso, with both wrists broken or bent, and the poles running down the outside of either arm.

To begin this flip, face up the hill with your back to the slope. Assume the correct pole grip and plant your poles in the snow on either side of your skis. To gain momentum to pull your body upside down, raise one of your legs and swing it up in back of you. As you snap the leg back to the ground and then through the poles, you'll need to pull up on your poles and tip the head back, spotting for the ground. Both legs will eventually leave the snow; all of your weight will be resting on your poles. The upper body, as it rises, tends to stay bent. Between 12 and one o'clock you must "kick out" or extend the legs and upper body to retain correct form. To do this think of simply shooting your legs out away from your body and straightening the bend in your waist. Try to lay out as early as one o'clock, then with a strong arm push, force your body away from your poles. This will complete the extension and set you up to land balanced on the balls of your feet.

Back Pole Flip with a Half Twist

To add a half twist to this maneuver you must wait until your body is extended as early as one o'clock if possible. With the body laid out and the legs pressed together to speed up the half twist, begin turning your head and shoulders in the direction you want to twist. Instead of continuing to watch the baskets of your poles, you must "spot," or look behind you. It's important that you push off your poles, otherwise the trailing shoulder can remain behind, thus blocking the turn.

When you find yourself parallel to the ground, look for the falline.

To add a full twist you must also begin when the body is laid out at one o'clock. Again, the head and shoulders lead. The arm push must be stronger in a full twist, and the legs closed. Both will help you acquire more height and spin faster, enabling you to fit in an extra half twist.

One Pole Pole Flip

A one pole pole flip is identical to a simple gut flip. There are a number of different ways to hold the free pole in this maneuver. You can twirl the free pole as you flip, or you can hold on to the other pole. However, it's easier to learn this maneuver if you take the free hand with the pole in it and grasp on to the planting pole, creating a "T." This requires less strength since you're able to hold yourself up with both arms instead of just one. Holding your poles in the "T" position, slide down the falline. To gain momentum for your pole plant, pull your upper body back, raising the front of your skis in the air. As you bring them back down to the snow, break slightly at the waist and plant one of your poles. At the same time, raise one of your legs and kick the heel over your head while watching the pole basket. The other leg will follow naturally. Match the trailing leg so that your body is completely perpendicular to the slope at 12 o'clock. Keep applying pressure on the planted pole, pushing your body away from the pole plant and toward the falline. Spot for the landing, keep your body extended, and bend the knees slightly for the landing.

One Pole Pole Flip with a Half Twist

A half twist can be initiated when the body is almost perpendicular to the slope. Instead of watching the baskets, turn the head and shoulder in the direction you desire to twist as you push off the pole.

CHAPTER 4

The Aerials

"In the air we do not feel any force of gravity. In modern parlance, we are weightless. Falling needs no explanation . . . it is the most natural thing that can happen to anyone. Only in avoiding falling does any force come into play. The weight you feel on the soles of your feet is pushing upwards, not downwards."

NIGEL CALDER

To leave the ground for which we are so specifically designed, if for just a moment, is to break the rules and test ourselves. Control, coordination, timing, grace, perfection. These words best describe the aerial event. And so upwards we push . . . for the feeling of weightlessness, for the freedom of flight.

What is it really like going off of an aerial jump for the first time, for the hundredth time? Adrenalin, "the

fight or flight" reflex, is pumping through your body. Your stomach is queasy, a thousand reasons to do something else will surface in your mind. It's terribly quiet; you can't hear anything. You concentrate only on your breathing, and balancing on the balls of your feet. You rehearse the take-off by lifting your arms and hips and turning your head. You ride the in-run, sometimes to determine the speed of the approach, sometimes because you can't stand the waiting. Someone pats you on the back, wishes you luck; you smile and give a wave without looking at him directly. You're ready, super-ready.

You look down the in-run and rehearse the next critical moments in your mind's eye, visualizing the lift created by reaching for the sky with arms, hips, toes. You imagine the feeling of weightlessness as you leave the lip of the jump and push upward. You experience a quality of timelessness when you've cleared the lip and it's just you and the force of gravity. Not only will it be absolutely quiet in this new dimension, but seconds will seem to turn into minutes, and you will feel as though you have all the time in the world to perform your maneuver.

The spell is broken as the technical delegate waves you on. Adrenalin. The aerialist chooses flight.

Looking at aerialists of the past you can see that many of the champions had similar body types. Jumpin' Jack Johnson, Jeff Chumas (both top five in the world in aerials throughout the 1970s), and Lea Hilgren (1977, 1978 Female World Aerial Champion) all had the tight, muscular, and somewhat smaller frame of a gymnast, which, as you might imagine, helped them spin faster. However, Eddy Lincoln (1977 World Aerial Champion), John Eaves (1978, 1979 Overall World Champion), Joanie Teorey (1977 Women's Aerial World Champion), and Marie Beddor (1979, 1980 Female World Aerial Champion) were equally coordinated in the air but were markedly taller and had larger frames. As always, there are exceptions to any rule.

If not body stature, what does it take to become a good aerialist? Two main things: physical skill and the proper mental attitude. You must be physically fit, for the mental decisions you make are transferred to the nerves and muscles within hundredths of seconds, and

the muscles must be able to respond. Mentally, you should feel confident and comfortable in the air. You should be able to concentrate and handle pressure in tense situations, blocking extraneous noise and action from your mind. This confidence increases gradually AS YOU GO THROUGH THE PROPER TRAINING STEPS. Diving, trampolining, mat work, and water ramping mixed with on-snow training is the only safe way to learn to handle the stress of competition.

Freestyle aerials have changed quite a bit since Stein Eriksen performed single front and back flips for spectators at Sun Valley in the 1950s. Eriksen probably never envisioned his shows becoming the catalyst for both amateur and professional aerial competition throughout the United States (and eventually the world) from the 1960s into the 1980s. But there it is. The Chevrolet Tour in the early Seventies added Eriksen's aerials at exhibitions of ballet tricks and mogul skiing.

In the early stages of competition, athletes were basically on their own as far as travel, lodging, and training were concerned. They built their own ramps and jumps and performed tricks that had never been done before. They coached each other with the help of videotapes and a good eye. Perhaps it was this struggle, though, that created the camaraderie that sustained aerials through the difficult years.

And aerials stayed! Stayed through the instant rise in popularity of the Chevy Tour from 1972 and 1973, through the Colgate Tour and Midas meets in 1975, through the 1976 battle between the Chevy Tour (the American Freestyle Skiers Association) and the Professional Freestyle Association, and finally through the insurance problems of 1978 which banished aerials, and the World Cup Tour with it, to Europe and Canada until 1983.

DRAG: Resistance of air to motion of an object through it depends both on the shape of the object and on the relative velocity between the object and air. The term drag is used for that component of force due to air directly resisting motion of an object through it. This force becomes more important as the velocity is increased, since for most shapes and velocities the force varies as the square of the velocity. For a given velocity, force depends on the amount of the streamlining effect by the shape and cross-sectional area in the direction of the motion. The human body in a crouched or tucked position meets with much smaller drag force at a given velocity than when standing erect.

Biomechanic Analysis of Sport

Yes, aerials stayed, but they did not stay the same. The single flips and Moebius performed by athletes like Hermann Goellner (1971 aerial champion, Waterville Valley, N.H.), Scotty Brooksbank (top combined freestyle skier from 1972 to 1979), and Marion Post (first woman to perform a back flip in competition in 1974) evolved into the triple flips of the late 1970s. The Eighties have now arrived. And the days of hiking up the mountain with a friend, shovel in hand, to build a ski jump are gone. With them is lost a bit of the spontaneity that endeared this event to so many freestylers

who were responsible for its remarkable growth. But replacing the single upright jumps and flips of the early Seventies are the multiple maneuvers of the Eighties.

Athletes link as many as five upright aerials together, and perform up to four flips with multiple twists in one jump. Spontaneity has been lost, and technology has taken its place. The result is a progressively exact, and infinitely safer event.

Because of updated training methods, expert coaching, and stringent qualification standards, upright and inverted aerials have reached a high level of perfection. Accomplished aerialists are gymnasts who have fine tuned body control, the result of long hours of mental and physical training.

Today, athletes are required to train for upright and inverted aerials on diving boards, trampolines, and water ramps year round. Individual progress is closely monitored by coaches, who are themselves former competitors. Once a maneuver has been mastered into water and the athlete feels at home in the air, the transition to snow is made. Each jump that an athlete performs in competition must be qualified in front of a technical committee before he is allowed to perform the jump in competition. Once in competition, maneuvers must be filed with the judges before the event. An athlete who performs a jump dangerously can be stripped of his qualification and be required to go through additional training.

A skier should approach learning aerials with the utmost respect. Safety must come before ego. The following pages will guide you through the basics of upright aerials, beginning with trail jumping. You'll learn how to become familiar with different parts of the jump before actually going off it, and then you'll be introduced GRADUALLY to increasingly difficult upright aerials. Some of the more advanced inverted aerials are shown at the end of the chapter; however, they are not accompanied by text. This is because inverted aerials should be learned under the supervision of trained coaches. For this reason an aspiring aerialist should attend a freestyle camp.

Learn the following jumps with split-second accuracy. Work on them until they become second nature. Practice under these guidelines; practice them over and over and over, and practice in a controlled environment . . . and push upwards, if for just an instant; leave the ground and experience the sensation of weightlessness, the freedom of flight!

Trail Jumping

Leaving the ground introduces a new dimension to skiing that is invigorating, challenging, and just plain fun; it is certainly the sign of an accomplished skier. Trail jumping is a good way to get used to traveling through the air with skis and boots on.

There are three types of trail jumping: transition trail jumping, mogul trail jumping, and natural hazard trail jumping. Transition trail jumping is done by popping off lips that are created by changes in the terrain of the ski slope, while mogul trail jumping is done in a mogul field. Mogul jumping is more spontaneous and requires greater coordination than transitional trail jumping, because on a mogul field the skier must take off with very little preparation and turn immediately upon landing. Natural hazard jumping, perhaps the most impressive of the three if only for the spectacular drops, is skiing off cornices and cliffs and in the woods. In this chapter we are going to cover transitional trail jumping. Mogul trail jumping was covered in the mogul chapter, and natural hazard trail jumping, due to its difficult nature, is not covered in this book. It should be learned in the presence of an expert skier or coach.

Transitions in a trail are the easiest and safest place to learn how to jump on skis if you don't have an aerial hill at your disposal. On intermediate and advanced slopes, there are points where the trail falls away abruptly. Usually, if the trail has been groomed, a small lip or crest will form where the slope changes in degree. By gaining a little speed before the transition, a skier can lift, or "pop," off the crest and become airborne.

Body positioning in the air is similar to that on snow. In fact, you can approach a transition and ride off of it holding the same stance through the air: head, shoulders, and hips pointing forward, hands held at nine and three o'clock with elbows slightly rounded, knees bent comfortably, and legs no more than shoulder width apart.

The Pop

To remain in the air a little longer, instead of simply riding off the crest of a transition, a pop (or extension of the whole body) occurs at the same moment that the skis leave the snow. As you may have guessed, popping requires a change in the basic stance.

You may recall that in the basic stance on snow the head, shoulders, and hips face forward squarely. The arms are held comfortably in view and the knees bent. This is the correct position for approaching a transition when trail jumping. To create the pop or lift, straighten the legs and simultaneously bring the arms up quickly from a 45 degree angle to the skis to anywhere from a 70 to a 90 degree angle. This transfers body weight and energy upward, and also straightens the body, making it balanced in the air . . . thus, the pop!

The rise in body position should begin gradually before the crest of the transition. As the skis reach the crest an upward, springing motion, combined with the straightening of the body, will make the body lift. If you are having trouble getting in the air, try increasing the speed of the approach, the strength of the arm lift, and the power in the leg extension.

REMEMBER: The approach and pop remain the same for all trail aerials except the helicopter.

Pop and Tuck

Once airborne, aerial maneuvers can be practiced, such as the tuck, and mule kick.

The first aerial maneuver to try off a trail transition after riding through the air a few times is a tuck jump. In the tuck jump, the knees are brought to the chest.

However, to tuck you must bend at the waist. The upper body leans over the front of the skis and the poles are tucked up and under the arm pits simulating the body position held by a downhill racer on the fast part of the course.

The thighs should rest against the chest, with the arms held tightly against the body. Press the elbows against the outside of the knees and rest the hands together directly in front of the knees and approximately one foot below the shoulders. Aerodynamically, this is the most efficient position.

It is possible to hold the tuck and still land in this position, or you may extend just before touching down. When landing in the tuck, the position must be held loosely so that the knees can absorb the impact by retracting up toward the chest.

The Pop and Mule Kick

When executing a mule kick, the torso remains upright and is held in the standard body position with the shoulders tipped back slightly. At the apex, or highest point in the jump, the legs are bent from the knee down, and the heels are brought back and up to the side, as if

trying to touch the back. The skis should be pointing toward the snow and the head turned slightly toward the side of the body that the skis are pulled to.

Trail jumping can help you make the transition to an aerial jump easier, that is true. But when all is said and done, in the end, it is just a great deal of fun.

The Aerial Jump

To make the transition from trail jumping to the upright aerial jump, you must become acquainted with the different parts of the jump. First, you should ski down the in-run and check the speed of the approach, the angle of the jump's lip and your body position. You should ski down the landing hill becoming familiar with its angle. By taking the time to do these things, you will become more familiar with the situation and the setting. Your confidence will increase, and you will be more relaxed—two factors which could ultimately protect you from mistake or injury.

Aerial Jump—USSA Uprights

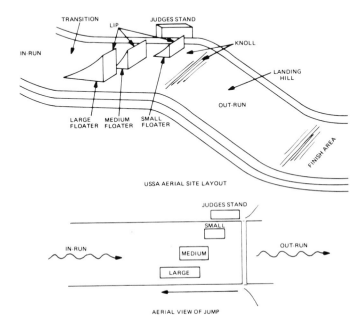

In-Run Body Position

Holding the correct in-run body position is important, for it is from this position that the pop and the aerial maneuver begin. If you are off balance on the in-run, you most certainly will be off balance in the air. On the in-run, the head should be centered between the shoulders, with the eyes spotting directly ahead, looking at the lip of the jump. Hold the arms well in view and slightly bent. This arm position may vary slightly with the individual, but it is safe to say that the arms are held somewhere within a 45 and 90 degree angle to the skis and well in view. The legs should be shoulder width apart with the knees bent in an athletic stance.

In-Run Ride and Speed Check

Practicing the in-run ride helps you get used to the approach to the lip of the jump. Use this time to familiarize yourself with the contour of the in-run and the consistency of the snow. With practice, this stance will become second nature.

Psychologically, this "quiet time" is important. It will help you to ultimately develop complete concentration and total relaxation. When you are taking your jump, you should be able to effectively block out all noise, both audible and visual.

Warming up with in-run rides should be done at the beginning of each practice session. Since temperature changes influence the speed of the approach, when they occur checks should be done at different points throughout the day.

To perform a speed check, ride down the in-run in the standard position. As you reach the transition of the jump, turn your skis sideways as if side-slipping up the lip. This will slow you down so that you don't accidentally ride off the jump, while giving you an idea of just how fast you should be going when you reach the jump.

Popping off of the Jump

Popping off of the aerial jump is very similar to the trail jumping pop. The mechanics of the leg extension and arm movement are the same as mentioned earlier: legs gradually straightened, arms moving from a 45 degree angle to the skis, then to 70 in an abrupt, lifting motion.

It is important to note that popping is tailored by the individual to some extent. While some people bring their arms directly up when creating a lift, others bring the arms in and up in a small semicircular motion. What's important is that the hands be out in front and that the body extend with the hips pushed slightly forward. This helps your body follow the contour of the transition before the pop and as you prepare to land. Find a style that works technically and that is comfortable for you.

One common error to look out for—be careful to drive your weight up through the hips and shoulders, not out. If your body weight is forced out in front, the chest will rest over the ski tips and balance will be lost forward.

In the Air

As the body travels through the air from the lip of the jump to the apex, it should be straight or "on axis." In other words, one should be able to draw a vertical line through the skier's head, hips, and feet.

Again, the eyes spot directly in front, rather than down, the arms are held in view, the legs are straight, and the hips are held squarely.

The Landing and Out-Run

After completing a maneuver in the air, you should close your jump, regaining the standard body position by closing the legs and bringing the elbows in toward the body with the hands resting out in front and slightly to the side. Make sure that the legs are straight and the

ankles and toes are pointing straight ahead. This will keep the skis parallel and out of danger of crossing as you land.

As you drop the last few feet before landing, look down at the out-run with the eyes, and the eyes only. It is incorrect to tip the head down while spotting the ground, since this can cause a loss of balance. As you make contact with the snow, the knees should bend to absorb the impact of the landing, with feet resting about shoulder width apart. At the same time, the arms should reach out in front of the body to help retain balance, for as the knees bend up on impact, the hips will drop back slightly. Forcing the arms out in front counters the sudden drop in the hips. Once the landing has been absorbed, a higher stance is taken, and the jump ends with a controlled stop.

Individual Maneuvers in the Air

Each individual maneuver should begin at the apex of the jump as the skier travels through the air. While this is especially true for single jumps, when double or triple upright moves are executed it is not uncommon to begin the first aerial a little early. The important point is that, with the exception of the helicopter, maneuvers are performed after the pop or extension from the lip and never as the skis leave the lip of the jump. Performing a trick off the lip without the proper pop is referred to as "slinging" a jump, and often indicates that the skier is scared.

Standard Body Position

Once the in-run, the speed of the approach, the lip of the jump, and the out-run have become familiar, it is time to ride off the jump. You should take your first jump in the standard body position as you did when trail jumping: head held high, body straight and facing forward, arms within peripheral vision, knees slightly bent and skis held parallel and close together, creating a right angle to the body axis. Remember, there is no pop in the standard body position when riding off the jump the first time, just extension. As you drop onto the out-run, let the knees bend easily and maintain

pressure in the front of your boot; this will keep your hips forward slightly. (See p. 85, "In the Air.")

The Spread Eagle

When performing a spread eagle, the upper body and hips remain square in the standard position, while the

arms and legs simultaneously spread out to the side and up, as if opening into a jumping jack.

The key to retaining balance in this jump lies in synchronizing the arm and leg movements. The limbs work as a unit, thus the width of the arm spread should be proportional to the width of the leg spread. The two motions counter each other and enable the skier to stay balanced despite the sudden action.

Timing of an arm or leg spread is a common problem in the execution of this jump. If one of the limb movements is early or late, it can tip the body, disrupting the axis of the jump. To prevent this, practice stretching or snapping the limbs out, then back in. Use your muscle power to do this, instead of extending the limbs lazily. This will help your timing, and it can transform a sloppy aerial into a dynamic one. Return to standard position before landing.

The Zudnik

The body position of a zudnik looks very similar to that of a nordic jumper in the air. In the zudnik, the upper body is held rigid but bent at the waist, and it is pushed out and over the tips of the skis. At the same time the legs, squeezed together, are brought forward and raised toward the upper torso. As the upper and lower body jackknife, the arms can be forced down behind the ankles, lying close to the sides of the body, or can be held in the standard position as seen here.

The key to performing this maneuver is to synchronize the jackknifing of the upper and lower body so that the motions neutralize each other. Think of trying to touch your chin to the tips of your skis. Be careful not to bend the knees in this jump, for this could cause the hips to drop back. The result: a loss of balance to the rear. To keep the legs straight, think of pulling the toes up while driving the heels down. This will lock the knees and enable you to perform the aerial cleanly. To land, pull the shoulders back and the heels down and return to standard position.

The Twister

The upper body can be held in two positions in a twister: a) the standard body position with arms out in front, or b) the standard body position for the head and hips, with arms and shoulders counter-rotating in the opposite direction of the twisting skis, as shown here.

Regardless of the arm position chosen, the upper body remains square and the legs are tightly pressed together with the knees locked. While looking ahead, the feet and skis are swung out to the side a minimum of 90 degrees to the body axis, then brought back to center in a quick, snapping motion.

The tips and the tails of the skis should remain perpendicular to the body axis; the feet lie flat. Holding the feet at an angle will change the angle of the skis, and proper form may be lost.

If the legs and feet are twisted to the side as far as possible, the motion will be stopped abruptly, blocked by the hips. This blocking almost "bounces" or "re-

bounds" the legs and feet back into the standard position, facing forward.

The Daffy

A daffy looks like a split in the air. With the upper body
in the standard position, one leg is brought forward and
up, while the other leg is simultaneously pulled back
and up. If the legs are split and extended correctly, the
skis should run parallel to one another: one ski pointing directly down toward the snow and the other up
toward the sky.

To retain balance and gain momentum for opening
and closing the maneuver, the arms can counter the
motion of the legs. If the right leg is brought forward
and up, it is balanced by raising the left arm forward
and up at the same time. As the left leg is pulled back
and up, the right arm trails with it. This is similar to the
rhythmic leg and arm movements of a cross-country

ski stride. The arms can also be brought out to the side
and up as you see here.

Because the tips and the tails of the skis are pointed
down, it is especially important to have a strong pop
for a daffy. If you are too low to the ground, you may
catch one of the skis. For the same reason, make sure
you close this jump a little early before touching down.
A lack of flexibility may prevent the legs from extending fully in this maneuver. However, with regular
stretching during dry land workouts, full extension can
be achieved, making this aerial one of the most exhilarating to do.

skis placed behind the hips, the shoulders should tip back slightly, and the hips should be pushed and tipped forward a little by arching the back.

The Mule Kick

The mule kick is a combination of a backscratcher and a side kick. The upper body is held in the standard position and the ski tips are dropped straight down into the same position as the backscratcher. Unlike the backscratcher, the calves and heels are right behind and to one side of the body, instead of being held directly behind the hips with the skis parallel to the back.

The Backscratcher

Similar to the tip drop, the backscratcher is done with legs closed and ski tips angled toward the snow. The variation lies in the degree that the ski tips are dropped and in the upper body position.

In a backscratcher, the upper body, hips, and upper thigh remain vertical. As the knees bend the heels of the feet are pulled back and up, creating a 90 degree angle between the thigh and the calf. This makes the ski tips point straight down and the tails of the skis run parallel behind them.

To counter-balance the weight of the boots and

A counter-balancing of the shoulder and hips is also necessary, with the shoulders pressed back and the hips pressed forward. The arms are usually raised above the head and the poles pointed up into the air. The head looks over the shoulder at the tails of the skis, again, aiding in counter-balancing the skis that have been brought to the side.

The Iron Cross

The iron cross is a combination of a tip drop and a tip cross. The tips of the skis should be angled down at least 45 degrees and crossed so that they create about a 90 degree angle. The upper body remains in the standard position with the shoulders tipped back ever so slightly.

The Helicopter

One of the most impressive of upright aerials is the helicopter. It is so named because the skier rotates 360

degrees on axis: the skis naturally follow the body and cut through the air looking something like a helicopter blade. The body is kept straight on axis throughout the jump. However, a number of different arm positions are possible: at the side, in front, clasped close to the body with hands at chest level, or over the head with hands together.

As mentioned earlier, when executing the helicopter, the pop is somewhat different due to the full twisting rotation. The twist, which initiates the 360 degree rotation, must begin as the skier leaves the lip of the jump. In some cases, the skier actually plants the pole on the lip of the jump to initiate the pop and twist.

The head, shoulders, and hips lead the body, which follows easily if it is rigid and the legs are closed. The more open the maneuver, the slower and possibly more sloppy the rotation. To keep from rotating too far, look for the out-run and, once around 360 degrees, open the arms to slow the rotation. Keep the head looking straight ahead.

Multiple Maneuvers

Once single maneuvers have been mastered, the next logical step is to try jumps linked together. A double trick can be a repetition of one trick (double spread eagle), a mixed trick (twister to a spread eagle), or a combination of the two (double twister to a daffy). Multiple maneuvers require more speed on the in-run, a stronger pop and clean execution. When linking

> **Once in the air, any twist of one portion of the body is counteracted by an equal but opposing twist of some other portion of the body.**
>
> *Biomechanic Analysis of Sport*
> NORTHRIP, LOGAN, McKINNEY

jumps, the skier should return to the standard position in the air before adding successive tricks. For example, a properly executed twister-spread is actually a twister, to standard body position, to spread eagle, and then closed.

CERTIFIED FREESTYLE CAMPS

Great Western Freestyle Center
Box 774483
Steamboat Springs, CO 80477
Phone Number (303)-879-4485
Owner - Park Smalley

Waterville Valley Summer Freestyle
The Mountain-Fare Inn
Box 553
Campton, NH 03223
Phone Number (603)-726-4283
Owner - Nick Preston

CHAPTER 5

Dry Land Training and Conditioning

Dry land training and conditioning are the backbone of every serious athlete's performance, and freestyle competitors are no exception. The better prepared your body is physically going into on-snow training, the quicker the coordination and timing specific to skiing will return. If you think you can "ski yourself back into shape" you're sadly mistaken, and run a high risk of starting the season with an injury. You must be in shape before you strap the boards on your feet in October, and this means dry land training beginning in early June until the snow flies. The U.S. Freestyle Ski Team training program consists of three parts: flexibility, strength, and endurance; all are equally important. Let's start with flexibility.

93

The ultraviolet part of the solar spectrum, especially the so-called UVA and AVB rays, are responsible for both tanning and skin damage. UVB, the burning rays, are the primary cause of sunburn and skin cancer and are most intense between 10 a.m. and 2 p.m. standard time. This is the time of day to avoid being out in the sun and, when you are out, to be sure to protect your skin. Altitude dramatically enhances UVB exposure, with a four percent increase in intensity for every 1,000 feet above sea level.

The New York Times

Flexibility

Flexibility is intimately related to overall health and fitness. Poor flexibility may cause bad posture, reduce work efficiency due to shortened muscles, and increase the risk of muscle and joint strain during athletic activities. Stretching to gain flexibility is an addition to your life style which you should consider seriously, and certainly not something to merely put up with before going out on the hill. This muscular-skeletal warm-up can guard you from injury, and improve your performance as well.

Before you warm up with the following stretches, make sure you understand these three points:

a) Stretch slowly, without bouncing, otherwise you could pull muscle fibers.

b) Stretch to where you feel slight discomfort, but no more. Hold this position for 20 seconds, let the muscles relax, and then stretch again, increasing the stress on the muscles just a hair.

c) Control your breathing. Try exhaling as you begin the stretch, breathe normally, and then inhale as you return to the start position.

For a skier, some of the more important muscle groups to stretch are hamstrings, quadriceps, Achilles' tendons, calves, lower back, groin, stomach, ankles, shoulders, and neck. Remember to start and end each training session with a good set of stretches.

Flexibility Stretches

Neck Bends

Standing with feet at shoulder width, slowly lower your head onto your chest, hold 10 seconds and return to straight position. Next, tip the head backward as far as possible and hold for 10 seconds, before returning to straight position. Then lower head to left shoulder, hold 10 seconds and return to straight position. Do the same toward right shoulder and hold for same time before returning. This stretches most of the neck muscles.

Shoulder Roll

Standing with legs at shoulder width and arms at your sides, lift one shoulder upward and rotate it backward; then repeat with the other shoulder. Alternate shoulders and then do them simultaneously.

Abdominals

TWISTER—Standing with feet at shoulder width, arms clasped behind the head, rotate head, then trunk,

clockwise so that you are looking over your right shoulder. Lead with head and allow arms to help pull you around. Return to starting position, then do the same to the left. Do alternately, holding each stretch for 20 seconds. This stretches abdominal and back muscles.

Lower Back

Lying on your back, bend your hip and knee and grasp the calf and pull it to your chest, holding 20 seconds and then releasing. Do not allow back to come too far off floor. Repeat with opposite leg. When finished, bring both legs together on chest and hold for 20 seconds. Do each leg a number of times, then both legs simultaneously.

Groin

GROIN STRETCH—Start upright with feet spread at shoulder width. Move left foot to the side, then shift body weight to left leg, bending left hip and knee while keeping right knee straight. Keep toes pointed straight ahead and stretch the inside of the right thigh; hold the position for 20 seconds. Repeat this to the right and do each a number of times to stretch groin muscles and those inside thigh.

V-GROIN STRETCH—Sitting on the floor, bring both of your heels together in front of you, so that the knees are pointing out. Keep the back straight, and gradually

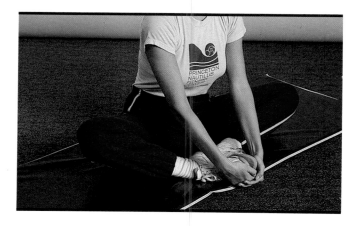

try to bring the heels in toward your body by pulling them in with your hands.

Hamstring

Seated on floor with legs straight, bend forward, knees straight, and attempt to touch toes. If you cannot straighten knees, forget about touching toes and concentrate instead on keeping legs straight by pushing them down onto the floor. Either way, be certain to stretch forward by bending to touch your toes; hold the stretch 20 seconds. Exhale while attempting to touch forward.

Quadriceps

Feet at shoulder width, bend right knee and raise right heel to your buttocks. Grasp right leg just above the ankle and pull backward, keeping it parallel to the left leg and not allowing it to swing outward. It is okay to use a standing object for balance. Hold the position 20 seconds and perform two times alternately. For an even greater stretch, lean body forward and attempt to pull leg parallel to floor.

Achilles

Stand with one leg in front of the other, bend left hip and knee so you are leaning forward onto it. Maintain back, or right leg with knee straight and heel down, to stretch that calf muscle. Hold 20 seconds and do alternately.

Strength

Strength can be developed in several ways. Two anaerobic methods of training used are weight training and plyometrics. If you're just beginning a weight training program, you should plan on lifting three days a week, every other day, for example: Monday, Wednesday, and Friday. Each exercise should be done with a weight that enables you to complete three sets, with eight to 12 repetitions in each set. Only when 12 repetitions become easy should you increase the weight. Work the major muscle groups first, moving from legs, to arms, to torso. Then use this same progression with the minor muscle groups. Abdominals, or stomach routines, are very important in freestyle skiing; much of the power in aerials, moguls, and ballet originates in the abdominals and the sleek muscles of the back. For this reason, stomach routines must be balanced with an equally good back routine.

If you don't have a background in weight training, see a trained professional at your local health club to get started. Once you're at the gym, remember to start these weight routines slowly, beginning each set with a warm-up of 10–12 repetitions using a very light weight. If you go at these routines "whole hog" from the beginning, you may be overtraining, some signs of which are fatigue, insomnia, and loss of appetite. Work hard and have some fun. Don't overdo it.

Ankle Circles

Sitting on the floor, pick up one of your legs and hook your arm underneath it, so that the foot is hanging in the air. With the opposite hand, grasp the ankle and slowly rotate it in a large circle, pulling the foot to each side as far as it will stretch. Change directions.

1. LEGS

LEG EXTENSION (for the quadriceps)—Sitting on the edge of the leg extension machine, hook your ankles under the rollers. Steady your upper body by grasping the sides of the bench, or the handles next to your hips. Fully extend your legs with the strength of the quadriceps until your knees lock. Pause in this position for one count, then lower the weights to the starting position. Repeat as required.

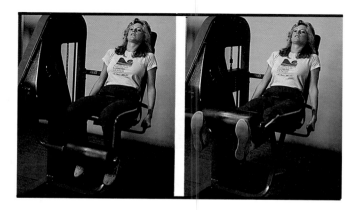

LEG CURLS (for the hamstrings)—Lying chest down on the leg curl table with your knees extending one or

two inches over the edge of the table, hook your heels under the rollers and grasp the edge of the bench in front of your head. Bend your knees as far as possible so that your heels are almost touching your backside, then lower to the starting position, and repeat as required.

LEG PRESS (for the upper thighs)—Sitting on the leg press seat, grasp the handles on either side of the seat and place your feet on the pedals in front of you so that your instep is centered. Push the pedals straight out until your knees are almost locked, then return to the starting position, and repeat as required.

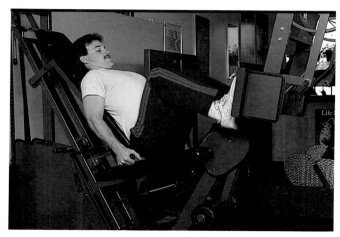

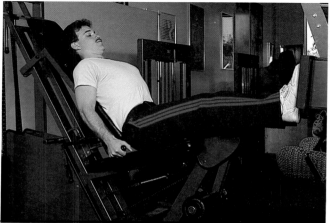

HEEL RAISES (for the calves)—Resting the balls of your feet on the edge of a step, let your heels drop and stretch as far down toward the floor as is comfortable. Then rise up on your toes as far as you can, using the muscles in your calf, and hold. Return to the starting position. To increase strength, you can place a weight on your shoulders. Repeat as required.

about a 30 degree angle, and interlace your fingers behind your head. Curl your torso up by bending the upper back, then the middle back, and finally the lower back off the floor, until your elbows touch your knees. Return to the starting position in the opposite sequence, and repeat as required.

(rotary)—These are done in the same way as above, the only difference being that, as you sit up, you twist the upper torso so that you touch an elbow to the alternate knee.

V-UPS—Lying on the floor, bring your upper and lower body up and together simultaneously, as if jackknifing.

2. TORSO

SIT-UPS (bent knee)—Lying down on your back, either on the floor or on an incline board, bend your knees at

Make sure that the back and the legs remain straight as they rise, then let the upper and lower body return to the beginning position slowly and repeat.

SIDE-UPS—Lying on your side with your feet secured underneath the foot pads of the Roman chair, interlace your fingers behind your head. Bend the upper body toward the hip without twisting. Think of trying to touch your elbow to your hip. Return slowly to the starting position, and begin again.

BACK RAISES (hyperextension)—Lying face down on the Roman chair, with your heels secured underneath the foot pads, slide forward until the top of your pelvis is directly over the front edge of the large pad. Interlace your fingers behind your head, and let your torso hang. Slowly raise your upper body until it is parallel to the legs. Do not raise the upper body above parallel, as this can strain the back. Then lower the upper body back down to the starting position, and begin again.

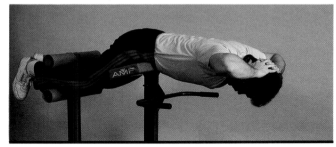

STIFF LEGGED DEAD-LIFT—Standing with your feet about shoulder width apart, bend at the waist and grasp the barbell resting on the floor so that the palms of your hands are facing your body, and are about two feet apart. Keep the knees locked and slowly bring your body up so that you are standing erect and the barbell is resting against your thighs. Make sure to do this exercise slowly, to avoid back strain. Once in the upright position, with your back straight, lower the barbell back down to the floor; repeat as necessary.

3. UPPER BODY

BENCH PRESS—Lying on a flat bench with your head at one end and your feet resting on the floor, take a hand grip on the barbell bar, palms facing forward. Support the barbell arms length above the body, directly over the chest. Bend the elbows and lower the barbell to your chest, then press the bar back to the starting position by straightening your arms, and repeat. A close grip will work the pectorals, a wide grip will tax the arms a little more.

INCLINE PRESS—Lying back on a 45 degree incline bench with your feet flat on the floor, again, take an overhand grip on two dumbbells, palms facing the body. Bring the weights down to the front of the base of your neck so that your elbows are pointing out. Push the weight straight up from the chest until your elbows lock, then lower the bar back down to repeat. There are a number of variations on this exercise. This specific one will work your shoulders and pectorals.

MILITARY PRESS—With feet about shoulder width apart and toes pointed slightly outward, take a shoulder width overhand grasp on the barbell as it lies on the floor. Bring the barbell to your shoulders by first straightening your legs and then standing erect. Raise the barbell until it rests at the base of your neck, across the front of your shoulders. Push the barbell straight up past your face until your elbows are locked and the weight is directly over your head. To return to the starting position, bend your elbows and slowly lower the weight back down to your shoulders, repeat. To return the weight to the floor after the required number of repetitions, bend the knees and then the waist.

BICEP CURLS—Sitting in the biceps Nautilus machine, with the seat adjusted to the proper position for your height, grasp the handles so that the palms of your hands are facing you. With your arms fully extended in the starting position, pull the handles up toward your face, being careful to keep your elbows on the pads. Curl your wrists to your chin as far as you are able, and then hold for a few seconds before returning to the beginning position. Repeat as required.

DIPS—Grip the ends of a set of parallel bars with your palms facing each other, and raise your body so that you are supporting your body weight on your arms as the elbows are locked, the arms, straight along either side of your body. Slowly bend your arms so that the elbows bend, but bend to the rear in back of the body, as your shoulders drop straight down between the bars. Drop your body as low as you can without losing control, then press yourself back up to the starting position, and repeat.

TRICEP EXTENSIONS—Sitting in the Nautilus arm machine with the seat adjusted for your height, flex and extend both arms to work the triceps. Hold extended for a moment or two, and then let the arms retract back in towards your body. Repeat.

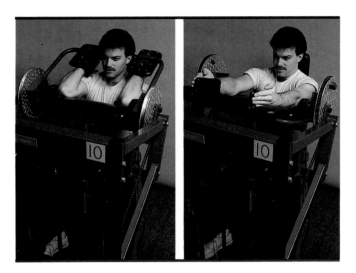

LAT PULLS—Sitting on the Lat Pull Down machine with your body strapped into the seat, grasp the handles hanging above your head, and slowly pull the bar down until it rests directly behind the nape of your

neck, as you lean forward. Hold, and then slowly let the bar back up to the starting position; begin again.

BENT OVER ROWS—Standing with your feet about shoulder width apart, grasp a barbell so that your hands are about two feet apart and your palms are facing your shins as you are bent at the waist, your back parallel to the floor. Pull the barbell up to your ribcage and hold, then return the barbell to the hanging position and repeat as required.

Plyometrics, a system of training adopted from the Russians, is designed to develop explosive quickness. The goal of plyometric, or "jump" training, is to increase elasticity and power in the major muscle groups of the legs and trunk. In skiing, many of the motions are similar to those practiced in plyometric training sessions, and the time restrictions of the exercises are similar to the times of competitive ski runs. Thus, athletes get used to "going all out" for up to two minutes, with a short rest between exercises. Due to the great amount of stress plyometrics can put on the muscles of the body, they are still a somewhat controversial form of athletic training. For this reason they are mentioned, and not described, in this chapter. The safest way to train with plyometrics is to do it under the guidance of a certified coach.

Endurance

Endurance is defined as the ability to withstand hardship or stress. Think of those last 30 seconds of a ballet run, or those last 15 moguls staring you in the face just before the finish . . . . Having the option of tapping an energy reserve and finishing your run in top form can mean the difference between 1st and 10th place.

Endurance, or aerobic fitness, is essential in this sport of freestyle skiing, and a strong aerobic base is the only way to approach the competitive season. Running and cycling are two terrific forms of exercise for dry land ski training. They tax the athlete cardiovascularly, while developing leg strength. As the summer draws to a close, interval training becomes a part of our aerobic program as well (see guidelines).

Interval Training Guidelines

INSTRUCTIONS—The object of this program is to develop power through explosive running. It is important to train to your maximum during these workouts to ensure the best results.

A few brief notes: Select a smooth area to run on, such as a football field or a track; avoid irregular terrain. Mark each distance below carefully, and then during the interval workouts, pace yourself so that you are able to complete the entire distance. The jog-rest is a mild jog back to the start line, while the walk-rest is a brisk walk recovery. Do not stop during the recovery periods. At no time should the recovery take more than three times the work time. For example, if you work for 30 seconds, take no more than 90 seconds to recover. Move immediately from one set to the next with a slight rest between each set.

PROGRAM #1

SET #1

4 x 25 yards work	25 yards jog-rest
4 x 50 yards work	50 yards jog-rest
4 x 25 yards work	25 yards jog-rest

SET #2

4 x 100 yards work	100 yards walk-rest
2 x 220 yards work	220 yards walk-rest

PROGRAM #2

SET #1

4 x 50 yards work	50 yards jog-rest
4 x 100 yards work	100 yards jog-rest

SET #2

4 x 220 yards work	220 yards jog-rest
4 x 440 yards work	440 yards walk-rest

PROGRAM #3

SET #1

4 x 25 yards work	25 yards jog-rest
3 x 50 yards work	50 yards jog-rest
2 x 75 yards work	75 yards jog-rest
1 x 100 yards work	100 yards walk-rest

REPEAT three times in all

Now that you are informed about flexibility, strength, and endurance, and how they fit into your training regime, here is a sample of the preseason conditioning routine for the U.S. Freestyle Ski Team. This is a guideline for beginner and avid competitor alike. Follow this at your own pace, and remember . . . enjoy yourself!

you've tucked away in the closet won't do you a bit of good if they aren't cared for correctly and often! Cutting corners to save a few dollars at this stage means a compromise in ski technique, which is hardly an even trade. Take the time to purchase the following for your tuning kit: a heavy body file, three mill bastard files (6″, 8″, 10″), a file card, a burr stone or sandpaper, two scrapers (metal, plastic), a few sticks of P-tex, some foam, plastic or newspaper, a roll of electrical or duct tape, ski wax, an iron, a cork for buffing, Scotch Brite, a true bar, and finally, a brake holder.

Most serious skiers buy a tool box to store these things in when at home or traveling by car. However, cloth kits can be bought from any major ski company, and are terrific to have when traveling by air where weight restrictions are enforced. Also, when traveling, the luxury of a complete tool kit is not always possible. You can get away with these bare essentials in a cloth kit: a heavy body file, a 10″ and 8″ mill bastard file, a file card, a stone, a metal scraper, a cork, and a stick of P-tex.

A HEAVY BODY FILE—is used for flat filing only. This takes the edge and the base of the ski down quickly, and should be used exclusively for skis that need a great deal of work, for example, those that are railed.

MILL BASTARD FILES—10", 8", and 6" files are used to produce different effects on the ski edge. As the size of the file decreases, the fineness of the "teeth" increases (similar to degrees of sandpaper). A 10" mill bastard is used mainly for flat filing in the early stages of tuning, although it can be used as a finish file when snow conditions are hard. An 8" file is a good "all around" file for daily tuning. A 6" file is best used on side edges, and occasionally as a finish file when snow conditions are soft or slightly sticky.

A FILE CARD—is a wire brush used to clean metal filings out of the teeth of the file. This increases the life of the file and the efficiency of the tuning.

A BURR STONE—is the same type of "stone" used to sharpen knives. It's rubbed along the ski edge to smooth out "burrs" which are irregularities, or little pieces of the edge, that are raised along the metal surface. If you run your finger along the edge of a ski you can feel the skin catch on these little slivers.

SANDPAPER—is used both to smooth out burrs in the ski edge, as well as remove base material from the bottom of the ski. Fine paper is used to dull the tip and the tail of the ski.

METAL AND PLASTIC SCRAPERS—are used for working on the base of the ski. The heavy metal scraper is used to take the base of the ski down when it is higher than the edge. Both scrapers are used in the last stages of ski tuning to take layers of wax off of the ski base.

P-TEX—is a skier's term for polyethylene, the base material of the ski which is in contact with the snow. It's sold in "sticks" or "candles," and is melted into the ski base to fill in gouges, restoring the running surface of the ski.

PLASTIC/FOAM/NEWSPAPER/TAPE—all come in handy for packing skis. Plastic, foam, or newspaper can be placed along the tips and tails to prevent nicks in the edges caused when the ski surfaces rub against each other. After wrapping, the skis can be immobilized by taping them together before placing them in the ski bag.

THE WAX AND SKI IRON—are used in the final stages of ski maintenance. Once the base and the edges of the ski have been attended to, ski wax is melted onto the base of the ski, then "ironed" into the polyethylene by running a warm iron along the length of the ski. This seals the base, prolonging its life, creating a smooth, extremely fast running surface.

A CORK—is used in waxing after the ski has been scraped. By buffing the base of a freshly waxed ski, you can make the running surface very fast.

SCOTCH BRITE—is an abrasive pad used for buffing and cleaning the base of the ski.

A TRUE BAR—is a metal "dowel" that has a perfectly straight surface, thus the word "true." This bar is placed across the base of the ski surface at different points, lying flush with the running surface. The condition of the ski base (convex, concave) or its edges (railed, beveled) can be determined by examining the amount of light that escapes between the surface of the true bar and the base of the ski.

A BRAKE HOLDER—keeps the ski brakes raised in the closed position, well above the ski base, making it easier to work on the edges. Nothing is more futile than trying to tune a ski with one hand while holding the brake closed with the other. Binding companies supply brake holders for their own specific systems. If these are lost you can use a rubber band or an old longthong, pulling it up over the heel of the binding and securing them in place.

The Set-Up

Tuning your skis in a work area makes the task much easier. All you really need is a workbench mounted with a ski vise at either end of the table. If the spot you've set aside is poorly lit, seeing the irregularities in the surface of the ski will be difficult. Rig up some temporary lighting if necessary by using an extension cord with a hanging lamp on the end.

Also, make sure that the area has an electrical outlet for the waxing iron. If music makes ski tuning less monotonous for you, set up a radio or tape player. The more enjoyable you make the work the more likely you are to spend time tuning your skis. For this reason, try to find an area that is heated. Cold hands make this task loathsome, resulting in a rush job. Ski tuning, like

any "hobby" that you do with tools, can become an enjoyable and peaceful pastime.

General Maintenance

Contrary to popular belief, new skis arriving from the factory are not "ready to go," though these conditions vary slightly with the manufacturer. The machines at the factories used for base grinding are automatic, and are not designed to fine tune a ski. Variations in new skis are quite common, taking the form of "railed edges," when the edges are higher than the base, and "concave" or "convex" bases, when the base of the ski is below or above the ski edge, respectively. Usually the ski manufacturer will suggest how the ski should be tuned.

Skis can arrive from the factory with one or all of these three characteristics. If a ski edge is higher than its base, it will not roll onto or off the edge easily; you'll have to fight to turn it. If the base is raised above the edge, the ski will pivot and feel squirrely or chattery underfoot.

To combat these problems, you must first know how to tell whether or not the skis are irregular. This is done by using the true bar. Place the true bar across the base of the ski at different points, from tip to tail, while holding the ski up toward a light source.

If the ski is railed, the true bar will sit above the base of the ski and light will escape between the base and the straight edge of the bar. The greater the amount of light escaping, the more railed the ski.

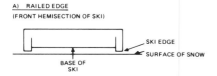

A) RAILED EDGE (FRONT HEMISECTION OF SKI)

If the ski has a concave base, light will escape beneath the straight edge of the true bar and the base in the middle of the ski, while the edges of the ski will lie flush. If the ski is convex, the middle of the ski base will lie flush with the true bar, while the edges will drop away and light will spill beneath either end of the bar.

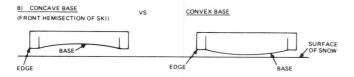

B) CONCAVE BASE (FRONT HEMISECTION OF SKI) VS CONVEX BASE

Flat Filing

To correct railed or convex ski bottoms, you can flatten the edges or base of the ski so that the two are flush. This can be done by either filing the edges down the same level as the base or by scraping the base of the ski until it is level with the edge.

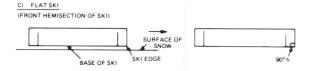

C) FLAT SKI (FRONT HEMISECTION OF SKI)

Flat filing a ski is relatively easy to do. If the edges of the ski are badly railed you'll want to use a heavy duty body file. This is the same type of file used in auto

body shops; it's a time-saver, and with two or three passes you can peel the metal edges down, then complete the tuning with a finer file.

Flat filing technique is the same regardless of the size or type of file used. Tightly secure the ski, base up, in a ski vise on the workbench. Remember, a file shaves metal in only one direction. When you draw the file from tip to tail, hold the "handle" or "tang" of the file in your left hand with the tang pointing up toward the tip of the ski. Place the file against the base at a 45 degree angle. Rest your thumbs lightly over the top of the file, directly over the edges, then apply an even amount of pressure as you draw it along the length of the ski.

You should be able to see and feel the file taking material from the edge of the ski. After every four or five strokes, wipe the shavings free from the base of the ski, otherwise these may become ground into the polyethylene. At the same time, take the wire brush and push the bristles through the grooves of the file, cleaning it of shavings.

For a person who has never tuned skis, some common mistakes are drawing the file across the ski in the wrong direction, from tail to tip, at the wrong angle, or with uneven pressure. Remember . . . tip to tail = t.l.u. (tang: left hand, pointing up!). Do not place the file perpendicular to the ski, but at a 45 degree angle. And finally, apply pressure on the file evenly over the edges of the ski, otherwise you unintentionally may "round" the edge.

Bringing the Base of the Ski Down

To flatten the base of a convex ski down to the level of the edges, you have to scrape away some of the base material. Ski shops are able to take the base down by running the ski along a stone grinder. You can do this by hand by running the metal scraper along the high points of the ski, shaving the polyethylene in sheets until the two surfaces are flat.

With both hands, tightly hold the scraper lengthwise, wrapping the fingers along the "back" of it and the thumbs pointing toward each other in front. Bow the scraper out very slightly by putting pressure on the thumbs as you push it along the surface of the ski from tip to tail. If you use even pressure and smooth strokes, the scraper will glide easily. If not, the scraper may skip, causing "waves" in the base of the ski. Scrapers, like many edged tools, may become dull, making this procedure difficult. You can sharpen the scraper by putting it in a vise and running a file along the edge of the metal card.

As you file the edges or scrape the bottom of the skis, keep checking your progress by laying the true bar across the ski base and examining the amount of

light escaping between the two surfaces. This will save you unnecessary work and will help you check your tuning technique. Remember to place the bar along the base of the ski at different points, for the tip of the ski may have a high base while the foot area may be railed. Work on these areas individually until the ski is flat. Once flat, it's time to square off the side edge of the ski, unless of course you wish to bevel first!

One Step Beyond
Flattening the Edge—
Beveling

Once the skis are flat it's possible to continue filing the edge, running the file at an angle to knock the square edge down a few degrees. Instead of a 90 degree angle the edge is "beveled" or "rounded" anywhere from 89.5 to 87 degrees. This may sound confusing, but a beveled ski is actually a ski with a convex base. The base is higher than the edges, and the ski is intentionally tuned in this fashion.

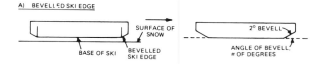

After emphasizing the importance of flattening the ski base and squaring the edge, why introduce you to a tuning technique which rounds the edges? Think about it. A slightly convex surface will roll on to edge more easily than a squared one. For this reason many slalom and mogul skiers have their edges beveled. This makes transferring from edge to edge in short radius turns quicker. With a flat edge you feel the whole length of the ski, and some people like the extra control of a bit more edge underneath them. Again, personal preference and style come into consideration when deciding whether or not to bevel, or how much. Most skiers bevel one-half to one degree although some bevel up

to 87 degrees. You must simply try the bevel at different cuts.

Years ago beveling was done with a body file. Unfortunately, this removed a lot of the base at the same time. Now with advanced tools the base can be left on, extending the life of the ski. You can have a ski shop bevel your skis on a stone grinder to the exact degree that you specify, or you can bevel them by hand in one of two ways: by taping one side of the file, or by beveling with a file holder that has a beveling adjustment.

To hand bevel, wrap one end of the mill bastard file with tape so that you'll be filing one edge of the ski at a time. The tape will raise the file slightly on one side, causing it to run along the opposite edge at an angle, rounding the edge. The problem with beveling by hand is that it is not as exact as a machine. If you bevel with tape wrapped around the file on one end, it's difficult to determine whether you've filed one degree or three. Beveling with a file holder is easy and exact. Simply adjust the degree setting on the side, and press it tightly against the base of the ski, running the file along the length as you would to flat file.

If you ski recreationally you may only need to bevel once a season. If you are a competitor, you may need to re-bevel once a week. Once the edges are flat or beveled to the degree that you want them and the base is even, it's time to side file.

Side Filing a Flat Edge

After flat filing a ski, side filing is done to square off the two edges. By running a file down the edge walls, you can smooth out any burrs which may have built up from flat filing or from being knocked about. This smoothes the edge, enabling it to respond beautifully to proper weight and pressure placed on the ski.

Side filing with a free hand is a little more difficult than flat filing because you have to balance the file along a thin surface, at a 90 degree angle to the base. At first this is awkward. To begin, place the ski on its edge in the vise and secure it. With the file in your hand, place your thumb and the heel of your palm along the top, curling the rest of your fingers along its underside.

From tip to tail, with the tang pointing toward the ski tip and the file resting parallel and flush with the side edge, draw the file evenly down the length of the ski. You can keep the file at a 90 degree angle to the ski edge by pressing the fingertips, which are curled under the file, lightly against the base of the ski. The base of the ski will guide the fingers along, allowing you to hold the file steady and square. As you apply pressure, metal filings will deposit along your index finger. Once again, as you work on the ski, keep the file and the ski base free of metal slivers by cleaning them regularly. (It's possible to use the file holder mentioned earlier, setting the degree indicator at 90 for a square edge, or at a lesser degree for a beveled edge.)

Complete this process on the side edges of each ski. One thing you may notice: if you're drawing the file from tip to tail, as you work on one of the edges you'll have to guide the file with the weak hand. This can feel very awkward, and at first you may make mistakes. With practice you can train your weak hand to be as coordinated as your strong one.

Side Filing a Beveled Edge

Side filing a beveled edge is a little more complicated than filing a flat edge. If you have a two degree bevel

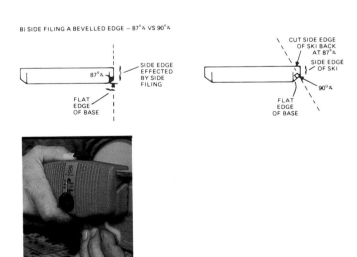

B) SIDE FILING A BEVELLED EDGE – 87°∡ VS 90°∡

87°∡ — SIDE EDGE EFFECTED BY SIDE FILING — FLAT EDGE OF BASE

CUT SIDE EDGE OF SKI BACK AT 87°∡ — SIDE EDGE OF SKI — 90°∡ — FLAT EDGE OF BASE

on a ski and try to side file as you would for a flat edge, you'll end up with an 88 degree angle instead of 90. To create a 90 degree angle you must "cut" the side edge back two degrees. This is possible by using the file holder shown earlier. You must adjust the degree setting on the front of the piece to coincide with the setting you beveled the edge when the ski was lying flat on the table, base up.

Finishing Touches on the Edges

To test the edges for sharpness, pull your fingernail across the edge of the ski. If a small surface layer of the nail is left along the edge, it's sharp! Do this down the entire length of the ski.

After flat and side filing are finished and the edges are sharp, it's time to take a whetstone and run it along the edges to eliminate any final burrs that could be left by the file. Run the stone along the side and flat edges of the ski lightly, making sure to keep the stone at a 90 degree angle by guiding it the same way that you did

the file when side filing. Curling the fingers under the stone, test again for sharpness using the nail test.

The final stage of filing is to dull the tip and the tail. Place the ski back in the vise so that the base is facing up. Take the stone and round the edge of the tip and the tail area at the point where the ski edge begins to curve. Leaving the tip or the tail sharp can be treacherous; the edges can catch easily and force you into a fall.

Waxing

Waxing helps seal the base of the ski and make it run more smoothly along the snow. An unwaxed ski leaves the polyethylene base exposed to the air, and oxidation occurs. In other words, the polyethylene molecules break down, causing the base of the ski to dry out and become slow. A layer of wax can seal the polyethylene base, prolonging the life and responsiveness of the ski. Waxes come color coded for different temperatures. To seal a new pair of skis, a specific base wax is used. You can find this in a ski shop. In the wax bag you will find temperature keys that help you decide which color to use.

For waxing, secure the ski base up in the ski vise. Set the iron on a moderate temperature, and with the point almost touching the ski base, press the stick of wax against the bottom of the iron. The wax will begin to melt and stream down to the tip of the iron. As this happens, run the tip of the iron up one side of the ski and down the other, leaving a thin stream of wax in a line on either side of the ski groove.

As a finishing touch, you may want to dull one or two inches of the edge along the front and back of the ski. This is largely personal preference, depending on both ski conditions and technique. For soft snow conditions you would want to dull the ski a couple of inches back at either end. For hard snow, it's best to leave a good burr. Thus, you may not want to dull much at all.

Experiment with this a little to find out how you like the ski to react. A sharp tip will almost whip you into a turn, a dull one will take longer to react. For slalom and mogul skiing, where quick carved turns are needed, the tips of the ski should be fairly sharp. Downhill skis are dulled extensively at either end, remaining sharp only in the foot area to prevent the skier from placing the ski on edge too quickly at a high speed.

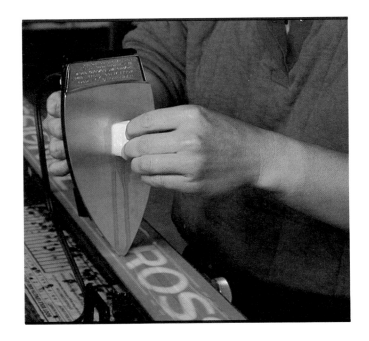

Next, push the iron slowly along the base of the ski, melting the stream of wax into the polyethylene. If you place the iron on a moderate temperature and keep it moving as it sits on the ski, there is no danger of burning the bottom.

Let the wax cool for a few moments, then take the scraper and remove most of the wax, scraping from tip to tail, leaving only a thin layer. Finally, remove the wax from the groove of the ski with a scraper or dull screwdriver and buff the base of the ski down with the cork until it shines. That's it! You're ready to slide.

Bringing Old Skis Back to Life

On an old pair of skis you will find gouges in the poly-ethylene, rust or burrs on the edges, and perhaps even a side edge pulled free. The tuning steps for an old ski are basically the same as with a new pair: identify the skis' specific problems by using the true bar, make the ski base flat by dropping the edge or the base, side file, and sand down any burrs or nicks in the edge. It's just that with an old pair of skis these steps may take a little longer. The difference is that before you work on the edges, you should inspect the base and fill gouges in the polyethylene with P-tex.

To fill in scratches in the base of the ski, first clean the bottom of grease and dirt by wiping it down with base cleaner. A common brand name is "Toko Base Cleaner." Wipe the ski down with the Scotch Brite pad. Once the bases are clean, take a close look at their condition. If the skis have been used at all, you will find some gouges in the polyethylene that have been caused by skiing over rocks or other hard materials. These should be filled in before the edge work is tackled.

Locate the dings that need filling and clean the dirt out of them by running the sharp edge of a knife or screwdriver through the gouges. Take the P-tex candle and the metal scraper over to the work table. Light the P-tex stick with a match and let it burn for a few moments until the black carbon has dripped free from the end of the candle. (You can catch the drippings on

If you're filling in a deep gouge, drip in one layer of P-tex and go on to another part of the ski. Come back and overfill the plug after it's had a chance to cool, sealing it with an additional layer of base material. Though it might not look like it, the flame and melting wax of the P-tex candle are incredibly hot. If the candle mistakenly drips onto cloth or paper it will burn a hole easily, and may even set the material on fire. Likewise, it can leave a painful blister on the skin. Use the metal scraper underneath the candle when moving from one area to another and you should have no problems.

When you've filled in all of the gouges and the material has cooled, run the metal scraper along the ski, shaving down the P-tex plugs so that the base is again flat. The sharper the scraper, the easier this step will be.

the scraper until you are ready to fill in the gouges.) If the carbon doesn't drip off easily, wipe it lightly against the edge of the scraper. Carbon dripped into the base of the ski will weaken the P-tex plug filling in the hole, and may cause the plug to fall out of the base.

Once the P-tex candle is burning with a blueish flame, move it over to the ski, catching the drippings on the metal scraper, and begin filling in the gouges by actually touching the candle to the base of the ski. If you hold the candle above the ski and drip the P-tex it will cause a build-up of carbon and the flame may become yellow and burn out of control. You must keep turning the candle so that the molten liquid burns evenly and slowly.

After the base has been repaired, tune the edges of the ski as you would a new pair. Rust on the edges can be filed off with a few passes of the mill bastard. There may be some unusually deep gouges in the edge; work on these areas with a file and stone, smoothing them out as much as possible. If the gouges are terribly deep, take the ski to a shop and have the technician run it over a belt grinder. This will take the edge down quickly, then you can file as you normally would. A "blown edge" or an edge that's pulled away from the ski, has to be fixed with epoxy. This is a somewhat involved process, which, for our purposes, can be left to a technician.

Traveling Tips

After taking the time to care for your skis, you'll want to do everything you can to protect them when traveling to the slopes. On day trips by bus or car if the skis have a chance of being knocked about en route, leave a heavy layer of wax on the bases when hot waxing. Then place plastic, foam, or newspaper between the two bases and tape the skis together so the edges won't grate across one another. This will protect the edges from becoming nicked. It also seals the bottoms from road salt and other foreign materials that can scratch or lodge in the polyethylene. And really, there's no

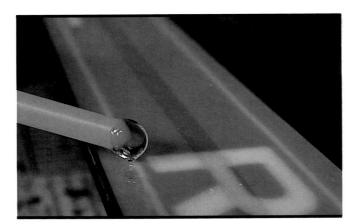

reason to scrape the wax until you're at the ski area. If possible, pack the skis in a ski bag when traveling. Otherwise, you can put them between the seats of your car if the weather is bad. You should pack your ski bag the same way when traveling by air. Throw a couple of elasticized cords in the bag so that you can secure it to a roof rack. This way you won't have to run about looking for rope at one o'clock in the morning.

A cloth tuning kit is really a must for traveling. Not only does it eliminate having to tote a tool box around, but it packs easily in the ski bag without causing damage when the bag is tossed around. Once at the mountain, simply scrape your skis with the plastic scraper, and off you go!

Specific Tuning for Mogul, Ballet, and Aerial Skis

MOGULS—Most high-level mogul skiers compete on slalom skis. Some mogul skiers, however, like a slightly softer ski with a "damp" shovel, or tip, because it bends a little more if you ski into the front of a mogul, where a stiffer tip tends to throw you. For the most part, mogul skis should be tuned like slalom skis. This is understandable, for from the waist down the two events are quite similar. Both require split-second decision making and immediate reaction. Both call for quick, short radius turns which begin by placing the ski tip on edge and carving through the turn.

The difference between slalom and mogul skiing is that mogul skiers roll onto the base of the ski and across to the opposite edge much quicker than slalom skiers because moguls are usually closer together than slalom gates. Also, during the absorption part of a mogul turn, there is a little more time spent on the base of the ski. Theoretically, mogul skiers should not use the tail of their ski as much as a slalom skier. Where a slalom skier accelerates out of a turn by placing weight on the tail of the ski, a mogul skier sets the edge of the ski against the side of the mogul, trying not to accelerate from the tail as much. The harder one

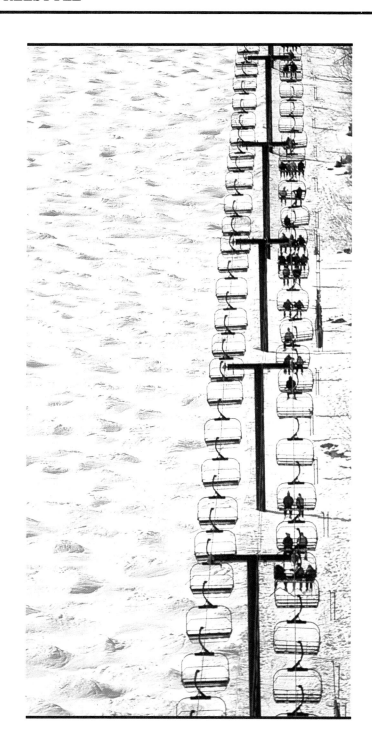

sets the edge on the slope of the mogul, the more controlled the speed of the turn.

Mogul skis can be filed flat or beveled, depending on personal preference. A beveled ski will roll onto edge quicker than a square edge. Try a beveled ski if given the chance. As for sharpening the skis for mogul skiing, follow the steps mentioned earlier. The only real difference is that you may want to dull the tip and the tail of the ski back about three inches. This will help it roll a little easier onto edge. But again, this depends on personal preference and ski conditions. If the snow is hard, don't dull back quite so far.

BALLET—Ballet skis are sharpened like a regular pair of skis. It's important that they're sharp, for the power that initiates rotations in the air depends on the strength of the edge set. A dull ski will slide into an edge set, and a great deal of force will be lost into the snow. With a sharp ski, a ballet skier can edge abruptly and transfer momentum and power straight up through his body. The higher a skier can clear the ground, the more rotations he can perform. As you can imagine, a poorly maintained ski can send a skier sprawling in the middle of a spin or linking step. Ballet skiers, probably more than any other type of alpine skier, are supremely aware of their edge. Like ice skaters, they create forms that depend on that edge, using the inside, outside, skiing backwards, landing with legs crossed, without a brake in line or balance.

Ballet skiers use a few different tuning techniques that are not edge related. For instance, most ballet skis are mounted by placing the ball of the foot on the center of the ski, then marking the placement of the heel and toe of the binding in relation to this. Mounting a ski this way places a little more pressure on the front of the ski, making it easier and quicker to transfer weight onto the ski tips. It also centers your weight along the ski, which makes rotational and spinning moves easier. Some ballet skiers like Bob Howard and Michael Russle, two of the world's top ballet skiers in

the late '70s, used to put a "tread" or "crosshatch" in the tip of the ski by heating up the tang of a mill bastard file and pushing it along the polyethylene, melting lines into the surface. This was supposed to increase friction between the ski tip and the snow, thus giving the skier more control. You don't see this very much these days, but apparently it works!

The earliest dated skis, found in the Fenno-Scandinavian bogs, have been dated to c. 2500 B.C. The earliest recorded military use was in Norway, in 1199, though it did not grow into a sport until 1843, in Tromso. Skiing was not introduced to the Alps until 1883.

Guinness Book of World Records

AERIALS—An aerial ski is used to get the skier from the top of the aerial in-run to the lip of the jump and then from the landing to a controlled stop in the bull pen area. For this reason, an aerial ski does not have to be as fine tuned as a ballet or mogul ski. It should, however, be well cared for. Make sure the ski is flat, stoned free of burrs, that the tip and tail are dulled, and that the correct wax is regularly applied to the base of the ski. A railed edge, a burr, or a sharp tip can place a skier off balance on the in-run or out-run of the jump. The consequences: an incorrect pop or landing, either of which creates a dangerous situation. Waxing is important for it makes the running surface of the ski uniform and fast, which will help you determine the correct speed for your approach to the jump.

CHAPTER 7

Nutrition: The Eating Edge

Thus far, you've been doing quite a bit of work with your body—dry land training routines, ballet maneuvers, aerials, and mogul skiing. However, a sound body, like a sound machine, doesn't run unless it has the correct fuel. This fuel, of course, is food, and the way in which the body functions depends on the type of food eaten, and how much and how often it is consumed.

This is one aspect of skiing that has do's and don'ts, and you should be particularly aware of the don'ts, because the dietary life of most competitive skiers runs counter to many sound nutritional principles. Since most skiers are up on the mountain from 8 a.m. to 4 p.m., they tend to either skip meals, eat them late and quickly, or eat those greasy foods which ski area lodges are infamous for serving. The great irony is that many a serious competitor's life style is devoid of the proper nutritional diet.

The key, obviously, is to eat a balanced diet and to be certain that your body receives all of the food properties needed to sustain its health. That requires some knowledge and planning, which will be outlined in this chapter. If you know what is involved in the three meals you consume each day, you will be better able to plan their nutritional content to fully complement your physical training. Let's begin with calories.

Calories

Simply stated, calories are a measure of the energy available to our bodies from the food we eat. This energy is required for the body to carry out all of its basic functions, such as digestion, breathing, maintenance of muscle tone, and regulation of body temperature, for growth and for physical activity.

That's the good news.

On the other hand, only a few of the many nutrients necessary for good health provide calories. Thus, weight control is the balancing factor . . . what you put in as calories versus what you expend as energy. To maintain your weight, your "ins" should equal your "outs"; to lose, your "outs" must exceed your "ins"; and to gain, your "ins" must be greater than the "outs."

Here's a good guide: The number of calories you must consume to maintain your weight can be calculated by multiplying your weight in pounds by 15, assuming you are moderately active. Thus, if you weigh 170 pounds, you require approximately 2,550 calories per day to hold that weight. If you consume fewer, you'll lose pounds; if you consume more, you'll gain.

Now, this is not a hard and fast rule. In some cases people have consumed fewer calories than the supposed number required to maintain their weight and still have gained—and vice versa. Generally, 3,500 calories equals one pound of fat. To lose a pound per week you must have a 3,500-calorie deficit, either in less intake or more exercise. Don't get greedy (pardon the pun) on the weightloss routine: One or two pounds per week is plenty.

You don't have to be a calorie counter, but be aware of them when you know you're going to have a big meal with all the trimmings—say, at Thanksgiving. Watch your eating carefully before and after the large meal. If you are mindful of calories and limit water retention by watching your salt intake you might be amazed at the extra pounds you can lose easily.

The levels of muscular contraction characteristic of most forms of Alpine skiing demand, for fuel, sugar stored as glycogen rather than as fat, and when sugar is depleted any skier's energy disappears, performance plummets, and injury becomes more likely. A skier's sugar levels can drop as much as half in a given day, and by as much as 80 percent over the course of a ski week.

DR. ROBERT ARNOT

Fats

Fats are the body's stockpile of fuel. Not all fat is bad—limited quantities are essential to everyone's diet. Still, it is estimated that 42 percent of our national diet is made up of fat. Fat content of 10 to 20 percent is reasonable and desirable if you exercise regularly. This is cause to check just how much you are ingesting each day.

Fat, as a condition, is Public Enemy No. 1 for people who wish to return to their attractive selves, but fat, as a substance for bodily well-being, has positive functions. These include:

1) A source of energy.
2) A source of essential fatty acid.
3) A carrier of fat-soluble vitamins.

You have heard much about the pros and cons of saturated and polyunsaturated fats, and how they relate to the dietary buzzword, "cholesterol." Saturated fats are believed to raise the level of cholesterol in the blood, which can lead to heart disease if it becomes too high. These saturated fats are solid at room temperature and can be found in butter, cream, beef fat, and in hydrogenated fats such as solid vegetable shortening. Other sources include palm oil, coconut oil, and cocoa butter. Polyunsaturated fats are found generally in liquid vegetable oils, such as corn oil and safflower oil. The good news here is that polyunsaturates tend to lower blood cholesterol levels.

Just what is this million-dollar word cholesterol? It is a fatlike substance produced by the body, and is also found in many of the foods we eat. Some cholesterol is necessary for many bodily functions, but excess levels are associated with increased risk of heart disease and atherosclerosis. The chief culprits are high cholesterol foods such as egg yolks and organ meats like liver.

One last note: The sources of fat include many obvious products such as butter, margarine, and oils. Other sources are fat not trimmed from fresh meat or within the meat itself, nuts, seeds, avocados, and poultry skin. The fat in poultry skin is the reason so many nutritionists advise skinning chicken before you cook it.

Protein

Protein—the name is derived from a Greek word that means "primary importance"— is essential for our diets, particularly for the formation, growth, maintenance, and repair of all bodily tissues. Protein supplies almost all of the nitrogen the body requires, nitrogen which can only be supplied by the food we eat. Many nutritionists advocate a diet of about 10 to 20 percent protein.

Recent research shows that while protein is the primary solid component of muscle tissue, and is used by the body to maintain muscle growth, it does not serve as an efficient energy fuel. In fact, protein is downright inefficient in this function. Thus, the old

Hilary Engisch—U.S.A., 1984 World Title, Tigne, France

wives' tale about having to eat a big steak before play-ing football was really off base. If anything, feeding a football team steak may hinder, not enhance, its performance.

Proteins are made up of amino acids. Eight of the 20 amino acids are essential, and those which our body cannot produce must come from our diet. Animal products, such as meat, have all the eight essential amino acids, and in the amounts our body requires. Plant proteins do not, hence the need to combine different foods such as beans and rice. When a good nutritionist puts together a "balanced diet," this is one of the considerations in advising certain combinations of foods.

Carbohydrates

Carbohydrates have come to be known as "carbos" since the marathon craze coined the phrase, "loading up with carbos." Carbohydrates are the third essential nutrient, and are usually the largest component of your diet. Their major function is to provide energy in the form of glucose, the body's preferred fuel. (The brain and central nervous system can only use glucose for energy.)

Simple sugars and starches are the two main types of carbohydrates. Simple sugars such as sucrose and cane sugar should be avoided because they provide calories but few nutrients. It is best to rely mainly on complex carbohydrates—whole-grain products, beans, and legumes—all of which provide many other nutrients and fiber along with carbohydrates. Our body uses carbohydrates in the following ways:

1) They may be metabolized immediately for energy.

2) They may be converted to glycogen and stored in the liver or muscle when intake exceeds the amount immediately needed. Glycogen is a reserve of carbohydrates which can be called upon as a source of glucose when needed. Marathoners always are concerned about glycogen levels, hence they "load up with carbos" up to four hours before a race to raise those levels as high as possible.

   Sudden depletion of glycogen is dangerous because it can cause numerous problems such as mood change, altered sleep patterns, even ruptured muscle tissue. The safest bet is to keep your diet continually high in carbohydrates and to couple it with regular exercise.

3) As with added calorie-producing nutrients, intake that far exceeds the body's needs can be converted into and stored as fat. You can increase your ability to store glycogen through regular exercise. Working out will deplete glycogen reserves, but if the workout is followed with a high-fiber meal that's not absorbed by the body, the glycogen reserves will quickly be restored.

Liquids

The importance of drinking enough liquid each day cannot be overstressed. Water is delicious with dinner and for athletes, is preferable to soft drinks, wine, beer, and liquor as a thirst quencher.

Water has a number of important functions within the body. First, about 70 percent of the body is comprised of water, and water is the principal solvent for other nutrients, carrying them to the tissues. While carrying away waste products, water acts as the medium for most bodily chemical reaction. It regulates body temperature. At rest, about one-quarter of your excess body heat is eliminated through water evaporation in the lungs and at the skin's surface. In hot weather and during strenuous exercise, much more water is evaporated in the same ways, and this cools you down.

With so much at stake, it is easy to see why we must replenish our body's water supply. How much water is enough? We eliminate a little over a quart per day in the form of urine. That much at least must be replaced, which means six to eight glasses per day, and more in hot weather and during exercise.

Exercise requires an increase in water consumption, and of course that goes against the old wives' tale that when you played certain sports such as football, you never took water during practice or a game lest you get stomach cramps. Doctors long since have found that the body needs liquid replenishment during these times.

Dehydration occurs when the body loses too much liquid during strenuous exercise, and one of the consequences of dehydration is muscle cramping. A natural thirst is nature's way of telling you it's time for a drink. But don't wait for that signal, particularly if you are training and competing regularly. By the time you feel thirsty, your body may be too dehydrated to perform at full capacity. Drink whether you're thirsty or not, and drink beyond feeling satiated during the strenuous periods.

Vitamins

Perhaps no other area of nutrition invites more dissension—and discussion—than the use of vitamin supplements. You probably heard about them from your parents during your earliest years. If you read the ingredient information on the food packages, you see vitamins listed; you hear about certain products which give you the "suggested daily minimum requirements." Magic is accorded to some products, healing is attributed to others, and prevention of anything from the common cold to leprosy, or so it would seem, is credited to still other vitamins.

What are these so-called elixirs of life?

The term "vitamine" was first used by a biochemist named Casimir Funk in 1912 to describe a substance both vital for life and containing nitrogen (amines). Scientists have since discovered the qualities and benefits of many different vitamins. Some of the most important ones are discussed below.

VITAMIN A—Aids night vision, or seeing any time when light is limited. It is necessary for normal tissue growth, and it helps to keep moist tissues healthy, especially passages of the nose and throat. A deficiency is marked by dry, cracked skin and dim vision. Vitamin A sources are identified by color: orange, dark green, or yellow. Vitamin A is fat-soluble, not water-soluble, meaning that it can be stored in the body. That is why taking supplements may be dangerous, and an overdose can be highly toxic.

B-COMPLEX VITAMINS—The B-complex is made up of many different vitamins. Let's make it easy. Here are some of their general functions and the foods in which they can be found:

First, the word "complex" in B-complex hints that these vitamins are complicated and wide-ranging in their function. They are a group of elements necessary for releasing energy in the body, and they work with enzymes to enable protein, fat, and carbohydrates to be metabolized. Some B-complex vitamins aid in preventing anemia. They occur in varying amounts in these foods: beans, whole grains, brown rice, wheat germ, green leaf vegetables, peas, lentils, brewer's yeast, meats (especially organ meats), and dairy products.

An excess of B-complex vitamins is generally thought to pass out of the body, and overdosing does not appear to pose the risks that can occur with overconsumption of vitamins A and D.

VITAMIN C, OR ASCORBIC ACID—Vitamin C helps to heal wounds, prevent infections, form bones and teeth, and strengthen some body tissues. Taking supplements of Vitamin C also is said to hold down the incidence of colds, but it is not a cure-all. Actually,

Vitamin C may make you feel better when you have a cold, but it cannot prevent you from catching one.

Vitamin C is water-soluble, meaning you must replenish it regularly, and since it's unstable in the presence of heat and oxygen, it is best to eat foods rich in Vitamin C raw and as fresh as possible. Sources of Vitamin C include citrus fruits, tomatoes, strawberries, raw peppers, raw spinach, watercress, and potatoes.

A deficiency of Vitamin C is marked by the symptoms of scurvy: loose teeth, bleeding gums, and very painful joints.

VITAMIN D—Vitamin D comes from three main sources: milk (Vitamin D is added by most milk manufacturers); bony fish such as sardines, salmon, and tuna; and sunlight. (Sunlight doesn't contain Vitamin D, but its effect causes the body to metabolize it.) Vitamin D will help to produce strong bones and teeth; it enables the body to use calcium and phosphorus, which are both essential to proper skeletal growth. A deficiency is marked by various bone and spinal deformities, causing a disease called "rickets," whose symptoms include bowlegs and "pigeon breast,"—a deformity of the chest.

VITAMIN E—Another controversial vitamin, Vitamin E has been credited with promoting sexual stamina, potency, and longevity, and is thought to be a safeguard against any number of diseases. Don't buy the claims because all are unproven!

But Vitamin E has been proven to be an antioxidant, and it helps prevent the breakdown of body tissues. Vitamin E occurs naturally in a number of foods already mentioned, particularly those providing A and B-complex vitamins. Some particularly rich Vitamin E foods include whole grains, wheat germ, green leafy vegetables, and vegetable oils.

VITAMIN SUPPLEMENTS—Consult a doctor or nutritionist if you believe you are vitamin-deficient. Don't walk into a health store and start loading up on supplements, and don't depend solely on the advice of those who sell the supplements. Loading up on unnecessary vitamins can be toxic if they are fat-soluble, and if they are water-soluble, it can give you the most expensive urine in town!

Minerals

If you eat adequate amounts of vitamin-rich foods, you'll probably get adequate doses of iron, calcium, phosphorus, magnesium, iodine, fluoride, sodium, potassium, and other "trace" elements. All are essential in varying ways, and all are needed in very small amounts. As with vitamins, if you follow a healthy diet, eating a variety of foods prepared so that vitamin and mineral loss is minimized, you probably will be assured of getting what you require.

Putting This Together

This seems like a lot to understand and apply. But one of the simplest ways to ensure that you are getting the necessary vitamins and minerals is to eat foods from the four basic food groups.

Foods with similar nutrient content may be grouped in one of four nutrient-based food groups: milk, meat, fruit-vegetable, and grain. Here are the main nutrients and foods found in each category:

MILK GROUP—This group contains milk and dairy products, including skim milk. Two servings per day from this group are recommended; 1 cup of skim milk or low-fat yogurt and 1½ ounces of low-fat cheese. Also included, if you wish, would be 1 cup of pudding, 1¾ cups of ice cream, and 2 cups of cottage cheese. Cheese can be considered as one serving in either the milk or the meat group, but not in both simultaneously.

MEAT GROUP—Eating less red than "white" meat is endorsed by most nutritionists. And when you do eat red meat, they insist, make it lean and eat only in small servings, not more than four to six ounces daily. But there are other products other than red meat in this group: veal, fish and shellfish, poultry, eggs, and legumes such as dry beans, peas, lentils, peanuts and

nuts. Skin the poultry to remove much of the fat. Don't eat oily fish, but if you must, cut down the portion; try broiling fish. Water-packed fish is better than oil-packed any day.

Among the psychological traits important to sports that have been isolated and tested are dominance, aggression, sociability, self-control, single-mindedness, persistence, acceptance of criticism, meanness, and anxiety.

DR. ROBERT ARNOT

GRAIN GROUP—Foods in this group supply carbohydrates, thiamin, iron, and niacin. The group includes all grains, such as barley, buckwheat, corn, oats, rice, rye, and wheat—and the bread, breakfast cereals, grits, noodles, and pasta products made from them. You are better off relying on whole grains, with a minimum four servings per day. What is a serving? One slice of bread . . . 1 cup of dry cereal . . . ½ cup of cooked cereal, rice, or pasta. You can increase the servings in this group proportionately with your calorie needs.

FRUIT-AND-VEGETABLE GROUP—Foods in this group supply Vitamins A and C, and include all fresh, canned, frozen, and dried fruits and vegetables, except dried beans and peas. Dried beans and peas, as we noted earlier, are in the meat group because they contain significant amounts of protein. Corn may be served as a vegetable, although corn grits and meal are in the grain group.

Your body requires a minimum of four servings from this group daily. A serving is ½ cup of vegetables or juice, 1 cup of raw fruit or vegetables, and a common portion of fruit such as a medium apple or banana. You also can increase this group proportionately with your individual needs.

One more type of food warrants our attention, namely junk food.

Obviously, the advice on junk food is to stay away from it. You certainly have seen a great variety of worthy substitutes which are much better for your health. Skiers are often at the mercy of the menus of base lodge cafeterias, which typically means greasy french fries and hamburgers. For some reason, these foods always seem to smell terrific! But BEWARE. It is possible to choose among the items offered and put together a healthy meal. For instance, most lodges serve

soups, sandwiches, milk, yogurt, and fruit. Try to control your craving for a nice, heavy burger.

Selecting the proper foods is up to you. Conscientiously cut down on high-fat foods such as pork, beef, and butter (and regular margarine is no better). Eat fruit for dessert. For variety try a fresh fruit compote. The juices from the fruits provide their own tasty topping. Don't use salt because a diet based on the food groups we've just discussed will contain sufficient sodium. To enliven a dish's flavor, add pepper or lemon and lime juice. These juices are great for melon. Also, mix them with garlic, onion, herbs, and spices for a salad dressing.

When you purchase food, read the label. You'll be surprised at how often salt and sugar are listed in the

ingredients. Avoid any product that has hidden salt and sugar, and in general think about preparing your meals from fresh ingredients instead of precooked or prepared foods. Using fresh meats, fruits, and vegetables is not difficult, but rather satisfying—as well as being eminently more nutritious.

Most of us, given the opportunity, like to take a turn around the kitchen. Once you begin and chalk up a few victories, the feeling becomes addictive. If you are competing and traveling at the same time, cooking can be difficult because the lodging may not always include a kitchen. But if it does, try planning a meal around carbohydrates instead of meat. Spaghetti and a low-fat sauce is a perfect example. Rice or beans can form the basis of other good meals. When you cook, it is best to poach, steam, bake, or broil your meat, fish, and poultry. Stir-fry or steam vegetables, or, if possible, eat them raw.

For you athletes who are trying to lose weight as well as train, the nutritional side of your diet is very important. It will take some willpower. None of us is too naive to realize that we may deviate from a new routine simply because the temptation is overpowering. There's nothing fatal in having a hamburger once in a while; no one is perfect, and you don't want to follow a course that makes daily living a grueling ordeal. Another tip: If you need to lose weight, rely more on low-calorie fruits and vegetables; if you need to gain, rely more on the higher-calorie grain products.

One final caveat regards alcohol and the use of caffeine. As a competitive skier, your life style may include many social obligations—sponsor dinners, cocktail parties, award ceremonies, not to mention your own social functions as a private individual. When you decided to become a serious athlete, you also took on the responsibility of fine tuning your body. Alcohol doesn't fit into this life style very well. If you're looking for a way out here, forget it. Remember, we have talked about moderation in our intake, and this also applies to alcohol consumption. Having one or two glasses of wine with dinner or at a social function well before a competition date might be okay, but you never know how it affects your performance until you stop drinking completely. If you feel as though you need a glass in your hand, go back to an old standby—water or club soda which may appear "more sociable." Again, this takes willpower—or actually—"won't power!" You must make up your mind that you are changing your life style. The benefits to society aside, if you feel you must succumb to social pressure to drink, go take a look in the mirror and ask yourself how much skiing to the best of your ability means to you. In addition, alcohol can severely dehydrate the body and, in even moderate amounts, attack vital organs such as the heart, liver, and kidneys.

If you are a coffee drinker, you certainly know about the stimulatory effects of caffeine. Should you cut it out of your diet? It seems safe to say that when you are competing, you should try to keep your routine the same as it has always been; it may relax you more to have a cup of coffee, which you enjoy, rather than a glass of water, at breakfast before an event. But again, moderation is a good idea, and as a rule, it probably is safer to limit your consumption of coffee to no more than two cups a day.

Decaffeinated coffee gives you more leeway, and now even restaurants are serving it brewed. Also, soft drinks now feature brands without caffeine, and tea also is manufactured with the caffeine removed. You can't go wrong following this course.

CHAPTER 8

How to Get Started in Competition

Freestyle skiing is not only for the world class athlete, it's for everyone. It has the beauty, showmanship, and self expression of the ballet event, the power, agility, and athleticism of the mogul event, and the precise, calculated timing of the aerial event. These three forms of skiing cover the spectrum of competitive athletics . . . here there is something for everyone.

And yet, it's difficult being the new kid on the block . . . but as you know, little happens when you stay within the confines of the backyard fence. Yes, it's safe there, of that you can be sure. Yet, to climb over the fence, to let yourself drop into the middle of a new environment feet first, is to grow and learn. When you move into unfamiliar settings, such as involving yourself in a new sport which blends team and individual

efforts as skiing does, you open the doors for self improvement, hopefully enriching others' lives as well as your own.

To get involved in a new sport takes both information and courage. The information gathering is the easy part, finding answers to those questions: Who do I write? How much does it cost? What do I need? Where do I go? These can be dealt with quite easily by making a few phone calls and by following the advice in this chapter. It's that first week of practice, when you actually "do" instead of "talk about," that's the tough part. For instance, those first few tricks that you try to learn from this book, or those first few mornings at the ski area when you're a new face among a group of old teammates, can be awkward. At first, you may feel as though simple mistakes are glaring major ones, and that everyone seems to be watching you when you make them! But you must realize that this is an exaggeration of the situation, and often the result of your own self-consciousness. Everyone began at some point, and you can be sure that they felt the same way. If you approach this new sport of freestyle skiing with concentration and a good sense of humor, you'll learn quickly and have a lot of fun at the same time.

Of the three disciplines, the mogul event is probably the most natural entry into skiing freestyle. If you've skied at all, you've skied moguls; they exist at every ski area across the nation. Entering a program which provides mogul instruction can only improve your overall ski technique, making skiing more fun and more exciting. This is a good way to consider freestyle as a sport and a good way to give it a go in competition. While you compete in moguls, you can train in ballet until you have learned enough to enter that event. Or, of course, you can begin with either ballet or aerials. A number of aerialists were not initially skiers, but rather gymnasts or divers. Many of today's ballet skiers had a history of dance or ice skating, which made the transition to freestyle skiing quite natural for them. A lot of athletes begin with one event, branch into all three, and then cut back and specialize in their one or two strongest ones. This has its advantages, giving the skier more time to focus and train in a certain area. Still, there are those freestylers who are talented enough to compete successfully in all three events!

To compete in freestyle skiing, you must contact the United States Ski Association (USSA). But what exactly is this association, and where does freestyle fit in? The USSA is the national governing body of skiing; it's recognized by Congress and the United States Olympic Committee as the sole organization overseeing all phases of skiing. It puts together programs for alpine, nordic, freestyle, and recreational skiers, and conducts events for juniors, masters, and officials of all ages and abilities. Freestyle skiing became a part of the United States Ski Association in 1981. At that time, representatives to the USSA Board of Directors were elected, thus giving freestyle a voice in the decision making process of amateur skiing in this country. The USSA acts as a parent association for the freestyle, alpine, and nordic associations. Each of these associations is run by a team of professionals who make decisions specific to their sport.

The USSA Freestyle Competition Committee is the governing body of amateur freestyle in the United States; it is organized in subcommittees such as Rules and Technical, Safety, Judges, National Teams, and FIS/Athlete Representatives. Other integral members of this association are the program director, who is responsible for everything from travel itineraries to team sponsorship, and the national and junior national team coaches, who not only train the athletes, but function as mentor, psychologist, friend, parent, negotiator, and travel guide! On the regional level, committees promote growth of the sport within their respective parts of the country, as well as to provide representation at the national level.

It's possible to excel in freestyle skiing at the state level and progress up the competition ladder, making it onto the Regional, National, World Cup, and ultimately, the Olympic Team. To begin, you must join the United States Ski Association. This requires paying a yearly membership fee which entitles you to a competitive license and monthly updates about the ski world. You'll be sent information regarding ski races, programs, and summer camps for skiers of all ages and abilities. Once licensed, you can enter regional competitions in and around your state, regardless of age,

ability, or experience. To enter individual events, you must pay a competition fee. This amount varies, but it is usually between $20 and $30 per event (as of 1985). As a new competitor in the East, you have to compete in the Qualifier Series, otherwise known as the "B's." This group is usually comprised of younger athletes from ages 6 to 15. If your ability is clearly above this level, sometimes within weeks of starting you can be moved up into the Championship Series. Known as the "A's," the Championship Series includes skiers sometimes as young as 11. In other divisions, everyone competes in the "A's."

You can compete in freestyle skiing regardless of your age, though you may find yourself surrounded by young kids at first. You can quickly progress if you have the ability. There have been extremely successful competitors at the World Cup level who have been as young as 15, such as Krista Pettibone, a top ballet skier, and as old as 32, such as Scotty Brooksbank, a former combined World Champion.

Each region conducts various types of competitions open to all USSA members. Check your regional calendar of events for listings. You will be competing in your particular age classification only.

Veterans II—40 years old or over
Veterans I—27 to 39 years old
Seniors—19 to 26 years old
Junior I—16 (and under) to 18 years old
Junior II—14 (and under) to 15 years old
Junior III—12 (and under) to 13 years old
Junior IV—10 (and under) to 11 years old
Junior V—9 years old and under

Regions across the United States are broken down in the following manner:

EASTERN DIVISION—Maine, New Hampshire, Vermont, Massachusetts, Connecticut, Rhode Island, New York, Pennsylvania, West Virginia, Virginia, Delaware, and Maryland.

SOUTHERN DIVISION—North Carolina, South Carolina, Tennessee, Arkansas, Mississippi, Alabama, Georgia, Florida, and Louisiana.

M.J. Tiampo—U.S.A., Park Smalley—U.S.A., Hilary Engisch—U.S.A.

CENTRAL DIVISION—Ohio, Kentucky, Indiana, Illinois, Michigan, Wisconsin, Minnesota, Iowa, Missouri, North Dakota, and parts of South Dakota.

ROCKY MOUNTAIN DIVISION—Nebraska, Kansas, Oklahoma, Texas, New Mexico, and Colorado.

NORTHERN DIVISION—Montana, Wyoming, and parts of South Dakota.

INTERMOUNTAIN DIVISION—Utah, parts of Idaho, Wyoming, and Nevada.

PACIFIC NORTHWEST DIVISION—Washington, Oregon, and parts of Idaho.

FAR WEST DIVISION—California, Arizona, and parts of Nevada.

ALASKA DIVISION—Alaska.

The different levels of competition are the Canadian American Series (Can-Ams), the National Championships, the FIS Junior Competitions, and the World Cup Tour. The Canadian American Series, still in its developmental stage, is conducted for the top American and Canadian freestyle skiers. Participants are selected to compete in this series based upon current regional results. Events are conducted in various divisions throughout the year, both in Canada and the United States.

The final event of the season, the National Championships, combine the U.S. Freestyle Ski Team and the top regional skiers from around the country in ballet, moguls, and aerial competition. Results from the event play an integral part in the team selection for the upcoming year. FIS Junior Competitions provide a

USSA Divisions/Freestyle

Jan Bucher—U.S.A. with a student

forum for international competition for the top junior freestyle skiers (ages 19 and under) from all participating nations in the world. The U.S. Freestyle Junior Ski Team is made up of 10 men and five women.

The World Cup represents the highest caliber of competition in freestyle skiing. Spanning approximately 10 countries such as Italy, Canada, and Sweden, the World Cup calendar commences in December and continues through March. Top national team skiers accumulate World Cup points, and their standings determine final season World Champion titles.

Equipment Needs

In alpine racing, each event—slalom, giant slalom, and downhill—requires a specific type of ski. The same is true in freestyle skiing. To compete in mogul, aerial, and ballet events, you'll need to purchase at least one pair of skis for each event. As extravagant as this may sound, it is necessary, for the events are quite different from one another. Mogul skiers compete on top-of-the-line racing or high performance recreational skis, depending on individual style, snow, and mogul varia-

tions. In the '70s, the length of mogul skis used to be significantly shorter than slalom skis. The decrease in length tended to make the skis chatter, vibrating against the surface of the snow; it also made them easier to swivel, rather than carve the ski, by swinging the hips through the turn. This led to the wilder ski techniques of the early '70s. Today the length of a mogul ski is comparable to that of a slalom ski; in other words, skis extend 1½ to 2 feet over the head. They typically have a narrow waist (which makes the ski quicker), and a somewhat softer tip (which aids in absorption).

Aerial skis are shorter than mogul skis by about 20 to 25 cm, with an optimum length rising about a half foot over the top of your head. The shorter length provides stability on the in-run and out-run of the jump, yet makes the skis lighter, so multiple maneuvers can be performed safely. Of course, the lighter the binding, the lighter the ski. The flex of skis varies with individual preference.

The floors and walls and the world they contained were graced with a sense of unreality. They seemed forever unreachable— a place, a culture, a history in which we could play no part.

In The Throne Room Of The Gods
GALEN ROWELL

Ballet skis are measured to just below the chin, right around the Adam's apple. Flex patterns of ballet skis, too, are highly individual. Some people use recreational models (softer), while others prefer junior racing models (stiffer). The poles used in ballet skiing are longer, about shoulder length, making it easier to clear the ground for jumps and pole flips. If you're just start-

U.S. Team, 1985

ing ballet, you can buy a long pair of regular poles, but these tend to bend or break easily. For this reason you'll need to purchase a pair of poles designed specifically for ballet skiing as you progress onto difficult maneuvers.

Most people enter freestyle events as part of a team, and therefore, are accompanied by a coach. Your coach will make sure that you are at the event early, and that you have the information you need to warm up on the courses before the event. If you aren't in a program, it's possible to compete as an "independent." In other words, you can ski in freestyle competitions representing yourself, rather than a specific team. This

is tougher to do psychologically, but sometimes it's necessary when there isn't a program in your area. Most skiers who do this are mogul competitors who train with expert skiers at an area that doesn't offer mogul coaching. It's very rare that a ballet or aerial skier trains alone because of the specialized nature of the events. For more information on freestyle programs and camps, see page 91.

If you must attend a freestyle event without a coach, either because you train alone or are the only person on your team who needs an extra competition under the belt, try to go through these steps methodically:

a) If traveling to the event takes over a couple of hours, arrive the night before. Events vary in length from one to three days, so call the ski area and find out the dates and directions in advance. (Some competitions are held at the ends of the earth—difficult to find!) On the morning of the event get to the lodge early. If you haven't checked in with the registration desk the evening before, you can do so the day of the event. Registration desks open up, at the very latest, by 8 a.m.

b) If you have competed before, you should have preregistered by mail well in advance to assure that you have a spot on the roster. Some meets fill up very early in the season (January). Check to see that your registration form was received at the desk. If you are a new competitor, you can register the morning of the competition. You'll need to bring the registration fee, which varies with each competition; your classification number, otherwise known as the license the USSA sends after you pay your dues; and the name of your regional affiliation (if you're from Vermont, for example, you're in the Eastern Region of the U.S.).

c) At the registration desk, pick up your bib. Then check with the organizers to find out what the running order is for that particular day. Competitors do not always run in the order of their bib number. For example, the first competitor may be number 40, rather than number 1, and the second, number 41.

d) Grab a trail map and find out exactly where the course is located. The people at the registration desk can mark the map for you. Ask when the training and starting times are for both runs, how the starter is going to count down, and what the specific course criteria are, if any.

e) Go to a corner of the lodge and stretch out.

Before you go up to the mogul, ballet, or aerial course, check your equipment, pack any extra articles of clothing or ski tuning tools in your knapsack, and drop it at the top of the course. It's a good idea to start warming up at least an hour and a half before the pace-setters are scheduled to run. During the first half hour, break the course or the jump into sections, studying it one piece at a time. Take notice of the snow conditions, the contour of the slope, the feel of your skis, your balance point, and the lighting. Memorize the course. If you're skiing in the mogul event, pick out the line you're going to ski and the bumps where you're going to do jumps. For ballet, map your routine out along the length of the slope, and study the spots where your difficult maneuvers are going to be. At the aerial jump, check the speed of the in-run, and the angle of the transition. Over the next hour, train lightly at first, then gradually increase the intensity of your training. Try a few runs or jumps at 95 percent. If you're having trouble, don't worry. Lots of times poor practice runs precede brilliance! If you're skiing great, let yourself feel good about it.

LONGEST RUN: The longest all-downhill ski run in the world is the *Weissfluhjoch-Kublis Parsenn* course (7.6 miles long), near Davos, Switzerland.

Guinness Book of World Records

Across the United States on the regional level, athletes are scored on a point system. At the beginning of each season, a score of 100 is given to the top competitor in each discipline from the previous year. When you enter a regional competition for the first time, you'll have a point total of 0! To receive a Freestyle Point System (FSP) rating, you have to compete in a minimum of two events over the course of one season. Scores from these first two events will be averaged to give you your FSP standing. They then are updated after each weekend that you compete. Not only do these points vary with the quality of your performance;

scored 18 in the same event, you would receive an FSP point of 68.57 {(18/20) × 80 = 68.57}. So to increase your points, it's a good idea to find out who else is going to the meet. The higher your points, the better your chances of selection for regional, and ultimately, the national competition.

How Long Does it Take to Become an Accomplished Freestyle Skier?

There is no magic formula for computing how long it will take to climb to the top of the freestyle ladder. Some overwhelmingly talented, emotionally tough skiers have skipped regional competition to ski internationally on the World Cup, taking the tour by surprise, then placing first to boot. Others have experienced the opposite, struggling, quite literally for years, putting up with disappointment, digging in, looking ahead to the next week, believing in their ability, feeling that their elusive goal must surely come. And come it did. Most of the top competitors began winning world titles when they were in their early twenties, and many are still winning seven years later.

Success is difficult to predict. Of one thing you can be sure, every world champion has had plenty of disappointments. Each has struggled, though it may appear otherwise to an outsider. Each has failed, picked himself up, brushed himself off, and gotten on with the task.

Everyone who has skied competitively has a story about what it was like getting started, going to that first event. When Hilary Engisch joined the U.S. Team and began competing internationally, she knew none of her teammates and had never traveled alone. She arrived in Geneva, Switzerland on a Thursday, grabbed her bags, and found a bus which was headed for Lac de Tigne, France that evening. Being the only person on the bus, she had plenty of time to contemplate what in the world she was doing there. Finally, three hours and 10,000 feet later, after passing through what seemed like hundreds of tiny French villages perched along

they also vary and are dependent on the caliber of skiers entered in the event. This means that freestyle events vary in "point-worthiness." Each competition has a different point value, depending on the points of the top 10 skiers. The top three FSP points of competitors who place in the top 10 in each event are averaged, and the resulting value is the Event Rating Point (ERP). The higher the ERP, the more FSP points you will receive for your performance! For example, if the winner of the mogul competition scored a 20 in an 80 point event, he would receive 80 FSP points. If you

narrow, winding passes that were barely wide enough for one car, let alone a post bus, she was dropped off underneath a street lamp in the treeless village of Tigne. There, she sat on top of her bags, watching the snow fall in the triangle of light cast from the lamp . . . "Eleven-thirty p.m., France. What in God's name have I done?" From a bar on the corner the faint sound of conversation rose into the snow-dampened evening. "What to do . . . a room, the U.S. Team, the event, am I even in the right spot?" She did what any respectable young person in distress would do, she sat there and cried.

Then a man and a woman emerged from the bar and strolled in her direction. Quickly picking up on four years of bastardized high school French, they realized that, not only was this little person upset; she was without a room for the night. They picked up the bags, took them to the bar, poured her a shot of the finest whiskey, then helped her upstairs to a small room. They tucked her in, kissed her twice on each cheek, as is customary in France, and told her they'd wake her in the morning.

The wake up call came early; the competition was that day. So, still tired from the travel and without time to train on the course—which is known as one of the most difficult, longest mogul runs on the tour, Engisch just showed up, unannounced and unknown, at the start. She won . . . both the race and the pleasure of having met two new friends who, in the future, she would return to visit each winter for the next five years.

This is a tough way to begin a skiing career, and most of you will not experience such difficult circumstances your first time out. But what you may find is that, as a competitor, you can be remarkably resilient under pressure; you may find that the more difficult the situation, the stronger you become. You also may experience the kindness of strangers, whether their hospitality takes the form of shelter for the night or simply a wish for good luck before your run. You'll never forget those moments.

You're not always going to be able to compete, or just ski, for that matter, under optimum conditions . . . . You may be injured, unprepared, late, ill, or thinking about things in your personal life. Two thoughts come to mind that have bearing on Hilary Engisch's story,

> **The steepest descent was performed by Sylvain Saudan (b. Lausanne, Switzerland, September 28, 1936), descending from Mont Blanc on the northeast side down the Couloir Gervasutti from 13,937 feet, on October 17, 1967, skiing gradients in excess of 60 degrees.**
>
> *Guinness Book of World Records*

and subsequently on your own. Involvement in this sport places you under pressure and, at the same time, introduces you to new places, new people. Concerning pressure . . . a sober and quiet mind must be able to be so in noisy situations. If you can do this, the rest is easy. And of the places, the people that this sport will bring you in contact with . . . be open to the world, its experiences, and its chance, rather than solely your intentions. Take these places and their people into your heart; in this way you will learn, and placing first will simply be the icing on a very rich, very fine cake.

CHAPTER 9

What You Need to Know about Judging

"The hardest part about judging? It's taking a sport like freestyle skiing and reducing it to points; this is really tough because the events and the athletes are so creative, and while judging is a constant . . . freestyle is not."

PAUL NICHOLAS
International Freestyle Judge

The evaluation of the three freestyle disciplines is done by a panel of judges, similar to ice skating, and the score that a competitor receives is a combination of objective and subjective criteria. Objectively, part of the overall score relies on speed in moguls, degree of difficulty in aerials and ballet, and compulsory moves

143

in moguls and ballet. Subjectively, the judges rate the execution of your performance in each event. Below, you'll find a review of national and international judging for moguls, ballet, and aerials.

By nature, each of us has a personal way of seeing, a preference of style. You may like the way a certain skier carves in the moguls, or the music and dance in a competitor's run, while your best friend may think the opposite. Judges can have similar disagreements . . . they're people, too, you know! So be prepared for "uneven appraisals," it's only human. Have confidence in the fact that the judges are following a set of criteria which is designed to complement all aspects of your event; the impersonal eye of the electronic clock used

exclusively in alpine racing is not the final judge in freestyle skiing. Have confidence in your own ability. Know what the judges are looking for before you enter the course—and try to give it to them, but keep your concerns for their scores in tow; don't be obsessed with them. Above all else, do the best that you can.

There are different sets of rules for national (USSA) and international (FIS) sanctioned events in each freestyle discipline. If you enter an FIS sanctioned competition, you'll find that the length of the courses, the running formats, and some of the judging criteria may be significantly different from those which you've competed under in the past.

National and International Mogul Judging

Of the three freestyle disciplines, mogul skiing is the most similar to alpine racing. Both rely on the technical perfection of carving the ski correctly, on skiing the right line, on speed, and on the dynamic, split second reactions of the athlete. In a way, though, mogul skiing is the purest of all competitive alpine skiing events. Everyone skis moguls; there's no need to set a course of bamboo to train. You only have to take the lift up the mountain and steer yourself to the top of a moguled trail. The style you develop from mogul skiing can be used universally, on all types of natural terrain. And, mogul skiing nicely blends the importance of speed and style, thus rounding the skier's ability by making it both aesthetically pleasing and technically fine.

Competitions take place on steep, heavily moguled courses. The judging criteria stresses carved technical turns, speed, and aerial maneuvers. These competitions can be judged in a single run format or by dual elimination, in which the winner of each round advances to the next, until first and second place are determined. In USSA sanctioned competitions, 60 percent of your mogul score is based on turns and line, 20 percent on air, and 20 percent on the speed of your run. In FIS sanctioned competitions, single elimination judging format, 50 percent of your score is evaluated on the technical quality of your turns, 25 percent of your score is based on the quality of your aerial maneuvers and landing, and the last 25 percent is based on the speed of your run. Attempts to create a universal set of judging criteria for national and international competition are under way, but no such standard exists today.

The technical turn in freestyle mogul skiing is a constant topic of debate, as are the biomechanics of turning in the alpine events of slalom, giant slalom (GS), and downhill. There are so many slight, individual differences in style, that definitions must be made with considerable caution. When a judge evaluates the quality of your mogul turn, a number of factors must be weighed. Some examples are the way in which the skis arch through the turn and the position of the upper body, arms, and hands. This is more complicated than it sounds because each of these technicalities depend upon the line taken, the quality of the snow, and the shape of the moguls. Let's look at what USSA and FIS judges will expect from you, as you set the ski on edge.

Pattern is his who can see beyond shape, life is his who can tell beyond words.

To receive a high score for the technical perfection of a carved turn, you must set the ski on edge when initiating the turn, then arch the ski completely through the turn and through the line that you are skiing. If you can stay on the snow as if pressing, or snaking, the skis through each turn, you will be using the ski and the mogul to their fullest. The radius of the carve turn depends on the spacing of the moguls, and the speed that you are skiing. In a tight course, it's necessary to shorten the radius of your turn. In a looser one, you must lengthen the radius. In a course which has deep troughs, you must absorb the bump with a flat ski, which can help you accelerate as well as remain balanced. It's complicated, as you can see .... There is no steadfast turning rule; the mechanics depend on body type, terrain, speed, snow conditions, and intention.

Regardless of the turning radius, if you're deflecting the skis across the falline beyond 45 to 50 degrees, chances are you're overturning. (Unless you are trying to get out of trouble, this technique can keep you from picking up speed, and may make your uphill ski heavy.) In the same vein, neither should you simply absorb the moguls, skiing straight down the slope without arching the skis back and forth across the falline. You see this when a skier is trying to go too fast for the mogul field. Unfortunately, in freestyle's dual skiing format, the speed of the skiers racing side by side can mistakenly become more important to an inexperienced judge than the quality of the skiers' turns. Competitors have coined the term "horse race!" to describe this type of skiing.

As a mogul skier, you should be able to ski the lines of the mogul field aggressively, but smoothly. The judges look for someone who is "digging in," or pushing himself to the limit, within the confines of the correct technique. (See the mogul chapter to review correct technique, page 9.) For example, you should keep a quiet upper body by absorbing the mogul, turning exclusively with the angulation of hip, knee, and ankle. Unnecessary movements of the hands and poles will decrease your score. Common problems are pulling the hand in across the body, lifting the hand above the shoulder for a pole plant, bending the wrist back and pointing the pole out, or continual double poling.

A judge looks for aerial maneuvers which are performed spontaneously. You'll receive a good score if you can perform a jump without being obvious, in other words, without spending a great deal of time setting up, or missing a couple of turns trying to regain control and rhythm after you've landed. Jumping on difficult parts of the course and remaining in the falline score higher than maneuvers performed in less difficult terrain and across the hill. Every competitor must perform two jumps, each from a different group. Under USSA rules, if two double maneuvers are done, they can't have the same group combination. For example, you can't do a twister-spread and a twister-kosack. All upright jumps are placed in the following groups:

1) Spread Eagle, Kosack, Tip Cross, Zudnik
2) Daffy, Splister
3) Twister
4) Helicopter

If you perform two different maneuvers which are difficult, correct in form, have a lot of height and distance, and a good landing, which leads directly into a carved turn, your evaluation will rise accordingly. Once again, jumps are categorized, and if you perform two aerials from the same category, you will only receive a score for one.

In events across the United States, either electric or hand timing is used to determine the competitor's

speed. (Hand timing obviously has its problems with accuracy.) In World Cup competition, the runs are always timed electronically.

You can increase your speed score significantly by practicing your starts in training sessions. Exploding out of the start gate not only is more efficient, but it sets the tempo for the whole run, both physically, and psychologically. When the judges see a competitor fire out of the starting gate, it catches their eye. In addition, the faster your run is, the harder you'll be pushing yourself. This will invariably affect how the judges score you on aggressiveness, plus you can improve your speed score by saving precious seconds with a strong start.

The speed score is calculated by taking a pace-setter time, giving it a point value, and then comparing all other times to this figure. The top three men and women from the previous week of competition paceset (run the course for time) before each new competition begins. The judges score these six runs on the quality of turns only; aerials, if performed, will be ignored. The course time of the male and female with the best turn scores will then be used as a constant in the speed calculation formula.

In nationally sanctioned events, the pace set time is given a point value of 4.5 (the maximum speed score being 6.0, which would be the total of three judges' maximum scores of 2.0). Individual times are calculated in the following way:

a) Each course time which is 3.125 percent above or below the paceset time is worth 0.3 points.
b) Times faster than the paceset time will be awarded scores greater than 4.5, but never higher than 6.0; those times lower than the paceset time will receive lower scores, but never lower than 0.

The USSA formula for calculating speed points is:

$$\text{Speed Score} = 14.1 - 9.6 \times \frac{\text{Competitor's time}}{\text{Pacesetter's time}}$$

The official paceset time for FIS sanctioned competitions always equals 5.625. Individual times are calculated in the following way:

a) Each course time which is 2½ percent above or below the paceset time is worth 0.3 points.
b) If your time is 2½ percent above the paceset time, you'll receive 0.3 points, which will be added to the constant of 5.625 awarded to the pacesetter. Similarly, if your time is 2½ percent below the paceset value of 5.625, 0.3 points will be subtracted from this number.
c) Regardless of how much you beat the paceset time, you cannot receive a speed score higher than 7.5; likewise, regardless of how slow you ski, you cannot receive a score lower than 0.

Example:

Paceset time = 24.53 seconds
24.53 seconds = 5.625 points
(75 percent of maximum points available)
2½ percent time increments = 0.613
(24.53 × .025 = 0.61325)

The speed points are then calculated by using The Grange Formula:

Speed Points = 17,625 − (12 × competitor's time divided by paceset time)

Judges do not have a rating system for falls within a mogul run. They evaluate the severity of the mistake subjectively and deduct points accordingly. For this reason, if you do lose control, you should try to fight the fall and continue your run, rather than give up as some competitors tend to do. Finishing a run strongly, even after a mistake, is the sign of a mature competitor, and a good sportsman. A competitor who throws a fit after a mistake doesn't help himself or his teammates. (We will always make mistakes; none of us are gods!) If you tend to throw tantrums, you should take a good look at yourself; hopefully you will see that your actions influence many people, and that you have an obligation to more than just yourself, regardless of the depth of your disappointment. Go off by yourself and do what you must—scream, beat your head against a tree—but return ready to engage with peers and friends alike.

The dual format of mogul judging in FIS competitions is used in the final elimination only (top eight women, top 16 men). It consists of two scoring methods, a traditional system and a rotational system. In both, the judges use the criteria mentioned earlier. However, instead of giving a score on a point system, each judge indicates the superior skier by holding up a flag, or card, that is the color of the course which was skied the best. In the traditional system, each judge scores turns, air, and speed, picking an overall winner based on the combination of these three factors. In the rotational system, each of the five judges has a specific judging responsibility which changes after each run. It sounds confusing, but it's really quite simple. One judge is responsible for rating air, one for speed (whoever finishes first), two for turns, and one for overall performance.

The dual format, while exceptionally exciting, does have its downfalls (no pun intended). The course you ski is determined by the toss of a coin. Unfortunately, the courses are never equal, and you may find yourself in the tough course, which is more difficult to carve, jump, and go fast in. While the other skier is cruising by in the course next to you with a great big grin on his face, having the run of his life, you can be having a miserable time, fighting to find the line and miss the rocks. Since you don't change courses with the same partner, there's nothing you can do about the difference in terrain but try to ski the best you can.

In duals, the ladder for the finals is determined by the semifinal runs; the first place skier from the morning competition skis against number 16. Another problem occurs when you run against one of the top skiers very early in the ladder. In single elimination, you might both be in the top four in the finals, even if one of you had a flaw in the semis. In duals, one of you will be knocked out in an early round, while a less competent skier in a different category may go on. These two examples, while not always "fair," are part of, that's right, "the luck of the draw!" Welcome to dual format skiing! A few additional notes: In duals, if you both lose your skis, the person whose ski first releases loses the run. Not so in the USSA, though you can put the ski back on and continue your run. In FIS rules, for both single and dual elimination, there are ski length limitations. A man must ski on 190 cm skis and above, a woman, 180 cm skis and above.

Ballet Judging

Ballet competitions at both the national and international level consist of two runs. At the national level, your final score is taken from your best of two runs. Internationally, only the top eight women and top 16 men from the semifinal run in the morning qualify for the final round in the afternoon. In the finals, the competitors have a clean slate. No points are carried over from the morning competition.

Although ballet skiing is performed on short skis, nationally, there are no ski length restrictions. Internationally, however, ski length restrictions vary with the height of the skier. (The FIS Ballet Ski Length Chart can be found on page 149.)

Ballet routines consist of jumps, spins, somersaults or pole flips, and linking steps that are choreographed to no more than two and a half minutes of music of the skier's choice. These four fundamentals are loosely defined as:

a) Jumps—are a variety of ballet moves in which the skier performs the maneuver in the air,

Meredith Gardner—CAN, Conny Kissling—SUI, Anna Fraser—CAN

F.I.S. Ballet Ski Length Requirements

SKIERS HEIGHT	MINIMUM SKI LENGTH
150 cm	121.5 cm
151 cm	122.3 cm
152 cm	123.1 cm
153 cm	123.9 cm
154 cm	124.7 cm
155 cm	125.5 cm
156 cm	126.3 cm
157 cm	127.1 cm
158 cm	127.9 cm
159 cm	128.7 cm
160 cm	129.6 cm
161 cm	130.4 cm
162 cm	131.2 cm
163 cm	132 cm
164 cm	132.8 cm
165 cm	133.7 cm
166 cm	134.5 cm
167 cm	135.3 cm
168 cm	136.1 cm
169 cm	136.9 cm
170 cm	137.7 cm
171 cm	138.5 cm
172 cm	139.3 cm
173 cm	140.1 cm
174 cm	140.9 cm
175 cm	141.8 cm
176 cm	142.6 cm
177 cm	143.4 cm
178 cm	144.2 cm
179 cm	145 cm
180 cm	145.8 cm
181 cm	146.6 cm
182 cm	147.4 cm
183 cm	148.2 cm
184 cm	149 cm
185 cm	149.9 cm
186 cm	150.7 cm
187 cm	151.5 cm
188 cm	152.3 cm
189 cm	153.1 cm
190 cm	153.9 cm
191 cm	154.7 cm
192 cm	155.5 cm
193 cm	156.3 cm
194 cm	157.1 cm
195 cm	157.9 cm
196 cm	158.7 cm
197 cm	159.5 cm
198 cm	160.3 cm
199 cm	161.1 cm
200 cm	162 cm

rotating around the vertical axis of the body. An example of a beginning rotation is a 180 or 360 degree rotation. Competitors on the World Cup level are performing up to 900 degree rotations.

b) Spins—are also done by rotating on a vertical axis, however, the skis remain on the snow during the entire rotation.

c) Somersaults or Pole Flips—refer to a variety of maneuvers in which the skier's feet leave the snow and the body rotates in a vertical axis over the head, in increments of 360 degrees.

d) Steps—are maneuvers which link all components of ballet skiing, and are the foundation of each ballet program.

Though the scoring systems vary greatly between the national and international levels, ballet judging is based on a universal set of concepts, namely choreography, technical difficulty, and overall performance. While scoring a routine in terms of choreography, a judge will listen carefully to the tempo of your music, paying particular notice to your ability to ski in time with the music, and to your interpretation of the music. An original program will make a stronger impression on a judge than a routine that is similar to others. Changes in pace within a routine that coincide with the music, as well as use of the body, pole, and ski "lines" to create illusion and mood, affect the score you receive in this category.

To approximate the degree of difficulty (DD) of your tricks, a judge will study individual and combination maneuvers as you perform your run, and then score your routine as a whole. If you miss a maneuver,

As they say around the poker table, the winners tell funny stories and the losers say, "Deal."

RED SMITH

you will not receive a DD score for that trick, however, your score for the overall performance will decrease in the execution category. In USSA sanctioned events, after a maneuver has been repeated twice and demoted by one category, if repeated again it will receive no points.

In the third category, overall performance, a judge will base his score on six factors: execution, utilization of space, chronological sequences, carriage, ease of movement, and virtuosity. When you execute jumps, spins, steps, and somersaults or pole flips, a judge will critically evaluate your precision of edge control, balance, and extension. Your score in this category will decrease if you stumble, lose control, have a break in body movement, or fall. During the execution of a jump, your ability to flow into and out of the maneuver, your height, the vertical axis of your body, and the tightness of rotation all play a large role in determining your score. To receive optimum points, you must finish your rotation in the air, landing softly, with proper absorption of the knees, and weight evenly distributed along the length of the ski.

To execute spins correctly, you should concentrate on rotating at a controlled speed, with the body well centered, creating an attractive line through carriage and form in various body positions. As with spins, you should emphasize line as you perform steps. A judge's score will be based on the level of coordination you display between all parts of your run. During somersaults or pole flips, the judge will study your ability to continue to move smoothly into and out of the flip, to hold a tight body position throughout the maneuver, and to perform twists at the correct point in the somersault. Somersault landings will be judged on softness and distribution of weight.

A judge looking at how you "utilize space" observes how you've mapped your run. If you've made good use of the dimensions of the rectangle, known as the course, and the vertical and horizontal planes of your body, your score should be high in this area. Putting a routine together is a deliberate process. It's important that all parts of your performance fit together smoothly, logically, and in an interesting manner. Take a look at a map of one of Jan Bucher's routines:

Sample Routine by Jan Bucher
(notice her use of the hill)

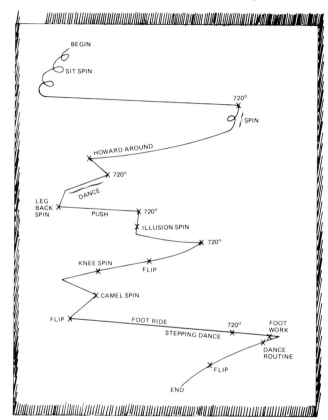

The finished plan should contain a balance of jumps, spins, steps, somersaults, and difficulty throughout the program. In addition, you will receive higher scores if you can perform tricks to both sides, and if your movements flow into one another, rather than stand as isolated tricks.

Carriage of the body can make or break a ballet routine. Actually, balance is completely dependent on the fine tuned positions of the body. The basic position in between dramatic poses or other theatrical positions is to stand comfortably erect. You should gracefully arch the back and hold the head high, so that it continues the line of the back. The legs, arms, hands, fingers, and poles, should be carried in a manner that will accentuate the beauty of your maneuver and the music which accompanies it. This is highly improvisational. Some of the gestures that cause judges to mark down scores are bent elbows (if unintentional, or not easily interpreted); a break in line due to arm, hand, or pole position; a dangling arm or leg; a dropped head; a bend at the waist; or a rigid body position. Your head and eyes should follow the direction of movement, the poles and fingers should be held easily, and the knees should be flexed comfortably between maneuvers.

If your routine is smooth and your maneuvers are performed with ease, harmony, and efficiency of motion, you can increase your scores. Learning to gain speed inconspicuously without poling or excessive foot movement can reduce lingering impressions of angular, violent movements. In judging, this is called "ease of movement." "Virtuosity" is the evaluation of your overall performance, technical skill, and showmanship. One last note concerning falling . . . while there are no automatic point deductions for falls or touchdowns, the judges will subjectively evaluate the degree to which the mistake interrupted your performance.

The scoring system for the ballet event used by the USSA runs on a point value system. Points are awarded

1984 World Cup Finals, Tigne, France

for composition and choreography in the following manner: 0.0 Not Skied; 0.5 Poor; 1.0 Below Average; 1.5 Average; 2.0 Very Good; 2.5 Excellent; 3.0 Perfect. These scores are combined with scores for the degree of difficulty of the tricks in a competitor's routine. There are six levels of degree of difficulty classified as A (least difficult)–H (most difficult).

Ballet scoring in FIS, like in the USSA, runs on a point system from one to 10. It is judged on choreography, which is 25 percent of the score; technical difficulty, also 25 percent of the score; and overall performance, comprising 50 percent of the score.

National and International Judging Criteria for Aerials

Judging of individual aerial maneuvers at the national level is similar to international judging; the difference lies in restrictions the USSA places on the courses (in this case, the aerial jumps), on the maneuvers allowed, and in the scoring system. In USSA sanctioned aerial competition, inverted aerials are not permitted. Since upright aerials are the only maneuvers performed, the jump site consists of floaters ranging in size from small to large (see page 83 for course specifications), rather than one floater and a number of front and back kickers, as you find in international competition.

USSA Rules

When scoring an upright aerial, USSA judges consider your execution from the time you cross the "upper no turn line" until you cross the "lower no turn line." They base your score on takeoff and air (the height and distance that you travel in the air), the execution of the aerial maneuver, and landing. During the takeoff, your balance, body position on the in-run, and pop will be studied. If you hold a nice basic in-run stance (see page 83), compress slightly by bending the knees, and then extend the body, popping off the lip of the jump, you should score well. As mentioned above, your air score is based upon the height you have at the apex of your jump, and the distance which you travel in the air. If your landing is short and you touch down on the knoll, the flat part of the jump at the top of the landing hill, chances are you'll receive a correspondingly low rating. (This is affectionately known as "knolling it.") By the same token, if you land down by the lodge, clearly below the designated landing area, you'll also be penalized! The maximum distance for landing upright aerials is 120 feet, which is usually marked with dye at the base of the out-run; this mark facilitates the judging, and is also there to help you know where "the optimum landing area" is.

As mentioned earlier, from the time that you leave the jump to the point just before you touch down, the judges will be scoring you on execution. Execution encompasses the precision of your performance, your stability in the air, and your timing. Precision refers to your form in the air. For example, part of your score will suffer if your upper body is bent incorrectly at the waist, or if your skis are apart or crossed during a twister. If you "walk" with your arms in the air by flailing them frantically, or if you tip off axis, it's a strong indication that your balance is not quite where it ought to be, and your stability score will drop. Each of these two factors, precision and stability, are intimately tied to timing. When you perform a maneuver or a number of maneuvers, the judges will expect you to complete half of the jump before you reach the apex. Another important aspect of timing is that each part of your jump is done rhythmically; during a double spread eagle, both of the spreads should be held for the same amount of time.

In upright aerials, a line is drawn across the top and the bottom of the aerial site; these are the upper and lower "no turn lines" mentioned earlier. The lower no turn line is about 120 feet from the knoll, or the top of the jump; it's where the judges stop scoring your landing. What they want to see is the proper standard body position right before you land, and smooth absorption of the landing with arms forward, and skis parallel (see page 85). Touchdowns and falls do not carry with them specific point deductions; the judges weigh the severity of the landing mistake on how it affects your jump as a whole. If you fall landing a spread eagle because you were facing backwards, with tails digging into the landing hill first, you'll be penalized more than if you had performed the spread facing forward, as you're supposed to, and simply caught an edge after you landed a perfect jump!

You'll receive a separate score for takeoff and air, execution, and landing; they are rated in the following manner:

"Air" Criteria

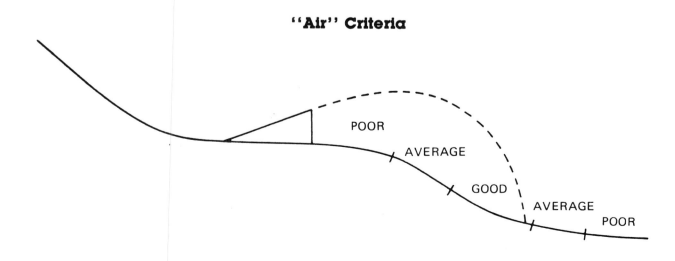

Takeoff and Air—Maximum: 2 points

0.0	Not Skied to Very Poor Trajectory
0.3	No Pop, Unbalanced, Poor Air
0.7	Below Average Takeoff and Air
1.0	Average Takeoff and Air
1.3	Good Takeoff and Air
1.7	Excellent Takeoff and Air
2.0	Perfect Pop, Balance, and Trajectory (Air)

Execution—Maximum: 5 points

0.0	Not Skied
1.0	Poor
2.0	Fair
3.0	Average
4.0	Good
5.0	Very Good–Excellent

Landing—Maximum: 3 points

0.0	Not Skied
0.5	Fall, Loss of Equipment
1.0	Fall, Continued Downhill, Standing
1.5	Severe Imbalance, Compression, Touch w/Hands
1.8	Moderate Imbalance/ Compression, No Touchdown
2.2	Slight Imbalance or Compression
2.6	Excellent Landing
3.0	Perfect Landing

Points from the three categories above are tabulated by dropping the high and the low score given by two of the five judges, then adding the remaining three to give the competitor a "raw" score. This is then multiplied by the degree of difficulty of the jump performed. Under USSA rules, you can only get maximum air points if you go off the large kicker. This is not so in international rules, where you can receive maximum points regardless of the size of the kicker you're jumping off.

International Judging Criteria for Aerials

The international rules for Junior National and World Cup competitions follow FIS guidelines. In the aerial competition, the event consists of two different acrobatic maneuvers in the air, from a prepared set of jumps. Each jump has a different degree of difficulty (for a list of these, please see p. 154). To score these jumps, the judges break down the execution of the maneuver into sections, as is done at the national level. Judges rate takeoff, height, and distance (referred to as air); proper style, execution, and precision of movement (referred to as form); and landing. Each judge's score is based upon a point system from one to 10, including 10ths of points between each whole number. (For example, a competitor could receive a score of 6.2.) A jump will be judged on three components:

a) Air—a maximum of two points, or 20 percent of the score per judge.
b) Form—a maximum of five points, or 50 percent of the score per judge.
c) Landing—a maximum of three points, or 30 percent of the score per judge.

Judges use specific criteria to evaluate each of these components above. By understanding these, you can train more efficiently, critically analyzing your own performance. You'll be able to learn how a correct jump feels, which should increase your confidence. When a judge looks down at the scoring sheet to rate your performance in the "air" category, he's considering the takeoff, height, and distance of your jump. Your height and distance rely on the speed of your approach and the strength of the pop. The takeoff is purely technique, and good form can be gained from repetition. These three considerations are rated in relation to the length and steepness of the landing hill. If you undershoot (landing on the knoll), or overshoot (landing on the

F.I.S. Degree of Difficulty Chart and Multipliers

	Degree of Difficulty Multiplier	Reference Number
4007.1 Uprights		
— Single	1.10	A-1
— Double	1.30	A-2
— Double Mixed (two different maneuvers)	1.35	A-3
— Triple	1.60	A-4
— Triple Mixed (sequential maneuvers must be different (i.e. daffy-spread-daffy, not daffy-daffy-spread; includes daffy-cross-daffy)	1.65	A-5
— Quad	1.90	A-6
— Quad Mixed (see note on triple mixed)	2.00	A-7
— Quint	2.30	A-8
— Quint Mixed (see note on triple mixed)	2.40	A-9
4007.2 Helicopters		
— 360	1.60	B-1
— 360 w/one pos.	1.80	B-2
— 720	2.20	B-3
— 720 w/one pos.	2.40	B-4
— 1080	2.90	B-5
— 1440	3.70	B-6
4007.3 Single Somersaults		
— Front Tuck or Pike	2.00	C-1
— Front Layout	2.15	C-2
— Back Tuck or Pike	1.95	C-3
— Back Layout	2.00	C-4
— Side Tuck or Pike	2.00	C-5
— Side Layout	2.15	C-6
4007.4 Double Somersaults		
— Front Tuck or Pike	2.75	D-1
— Front Layout–Tuck	2.90	D-2
— Front Layout–Layout	3.05	D-3
— Back Tuck or Pike	2.60	D-4
— Back Layout–Tuck	2.65	D-5
— Back Layout–Layout	2.70	D-6
4007.5 Triple Somersaults		
— Front Tuck or Pike	3.65	E-1
— Front Layout–Tuck–Tuck	3.80	E-2
— Front Layout–Layout–Tuck	3.95	E-3
— Front Layout–Layout–Lay	4.10	E-4
— Back Tuck or Pike	3.30	E-5
— Back Layout–Tuck–Tuck	3.35	E-6
— Back Layout–Layout–Tuck	3.40	E-7
— Back Layout–Layout–Lay	3.45	E-8

	Degree of Difficulty Multiplier	Reference Number
4007.6　Single Somersaults w/Twists		
— Front w/Single Twist	2.45	F-1
— Front w/Double Twist	2.95	F-2
— Back w/Single Twist	2.30	F-3
— Back w/Double Twist	2.80	F-4
4007.7　Double Somersaults w/Twists		
— Front w/Single Twist–Single Tuck	3.20	G-1
— Front w/Single Twist–Layout	3.35	G-2
— Front Full In–Full Out	3.65	G-3
— Front Tuck In–Double Full Out	3.70	G-4
— Front Layout In–Double Full Out	3.85	G-5
— Front Half In–Half Out (Tuck Position)	3.05	G-6
— Back w/Single Twist–Single Tuck	2.95	G-7
— Back Half In–Half Out (Tuck Position)	2.90	G-8
— Back w/Single Twist–Layout	3.00	G-9
— Back Half In–Half Out (Tuck Position)	3.00	G-10
— Back Full In–Full Out	3.30	G-11
— Back Half In–1½ Out	3.40	G-12
— Back 1½ In–Half Out	3.40	G-13
— Back Tuck In–Double Full Out	3.45	G-14
— Back Layout In–Double Full Out	3.50	G-15
— Back Full In–Double Full Out	3.80	G-16
— Back Full In–Full Out	3.80	G-17
— Back Double Full In–Full Out	3.80	G-18
— Back Half In–2½ Out	3.90	G-19
— Back 2½ In–½ Out	3.90	G-20
— Back Layout In–Triple Full Out	4.00	G-21
— Back Triple Full In–Layout Out	4.00	G-22
— Back In–Quad Twist Out	4.50	G-23
4007.8　Triple Somersaults w/Twists		
— Front w/Single Twist–Tuck–Tuck	4.10	H-1
— Front w/Single Twist–Single Twist–Tuck	4.55	H-2
— Back w/Single Twist–Tuck–Tuck	3.65	H-3
— Back w/Single Twist–Layout–Tuck	3.70	H-4
— Back w/Single Twist–Layout–Layout	3.75	H-5
— Back Layout Half In–Half Out	3.65	H-6
— Back w/Single Twist–Single Twist–Tuck	4.00	H-7
— Back w/Single Twist–Single Twist–Single	4.35	H-8

flats, beyond the transition) the jump, your score will suffer. Individual jumps vary quite a bit, so it's important to get in as much training time as possible, for the competition jump can be markedly different from the one that you trained on the week before.

In the "form" category, the judge will rate you on the position of your hands, arms, body, skis, and poles in the air. He is looking for precision: the tightness of your body position, economy of motion, balance, and timing of the maneuver in relation to the apex of the jump.

The landing category score involves the time immediately before the landing to a point at which the competitor has shown sufficient control on the out-run. This is subjective, but the transition from landing to stable body position (parallel) usually takes about four to five seconds. You do not have to come to a controlled stop; if you catch an edge at the bottom of the outrun it will not affect your score. When you absorb during the impact of the landing, the judges will penalize you if you bend at the waist, instead of absorbing with the knees and lower body. If you fall or touch down during a landing, the judges will drop their scores in proportion to the severity of the mistake.

You may run across a few limitations in international competition, such as qualification, licenses, and age. In competition, you must perform jumps that have been previously qualified before a technical committee. During the season if you wish to raise your degree of difficulty to increase your scores, it's possible to qualify a new jump before an FIS technical authority. Your national association or FIS representative will issue you a license listing the maneuvers that you're qualified to perform in competition. However, this license can be suspended or annulled if you are unable to safely perform the maneuvers listed. In addition, age limitations also exist, and follow this format:

Youth I—Uprights only—up to 13th birthday in competition year.
Youth II—Single Inverteds—14th and 15th birthday in competition year.
Juniors—Double Inverteds—16th, 17th, and 18th birthday in competition year.

Louise Barma, F.I.S. judge

Seniors—Triple Inverteds—19th birthday in competition year.

The calendar year begins on the first of July. Youth II, Juniors, and Seniors are allowed to compete in World Cup Competitions if they have turned 15 by July 1st of that season.

Perhaps now you can appreciate all that goes into

the score you see next to your name on the result sheet. Imagine yourself as a judge, think of the diversity of the events and of the styles from competitor to competitor. Think of the responsibility, the concentration you must retain over long periods of time, and under varying weather conditions, and you may realize that . . .

"The intensity of the sport ultimately relies upon the integrity of the judges."

GEORGE COMB
1984 National Judges Clinic

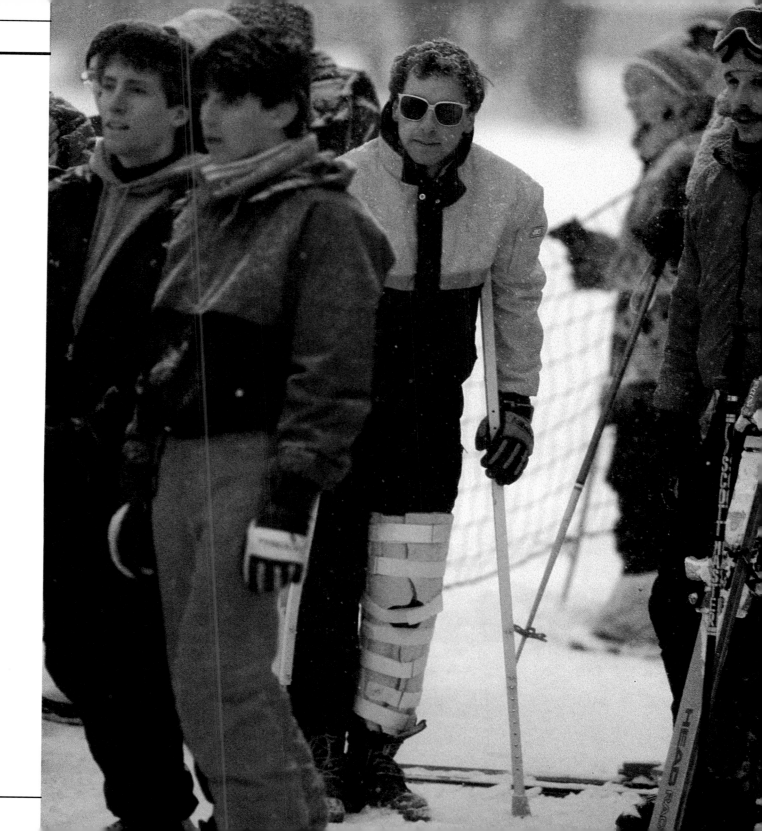

neurologist can diagnose the symptoms by conducting a series of tests. Unfortunately, rest for four to six weeks is the form of treatment for this nerve injury, in addition to anti-inflammatories. If the condition keeps coming back, it may be necessary to move the nerve surgically.

SPRAINED WRIST—In the ballet and mogul event, a great deal of pressure is placed on the wrist during the pole plant. However, the wrist is not designed to be a weight bearing joint, and thus, sprains can occur. You may sprain the wrist when it is forced to bend beyond its normal range of motion, stretching or damaging the ligaments or joint capsule. During a ski fall, the wrist is usually forced back toward the forearm. Although a sprain is not a serious injury, it can be very painful. Swelling develops almost immediately in the area around the injured ligament; discoloration from small amounts of bleeding into the tissues can also occur. To ensure that the wrist has a chance to rest, it should first be wrapped with an Ace bandage to reduce the swelling, and then immobilized in a splint. A bad sprain can take up to six weeks for the scar tissue to form between the rip in the ligament, while a minor sprain can heal within one week.

SPRAINED FINGERS—Finger sprains are categorized by degree of severity. A grade one sprain is a slight tear of the ligament, a grade two tear is a bit more serious, damaging sometimes more than half of the ligament, and a grade three sprain is a complete tear. The ligaments of the fingers run within the joint capsule which covers the individual bones in the hand. As mentioned earlier, sprains swell a great deal, resulting in both discomfort and inhibition of the normal range of motion. You treat sprained fingers like other sprains, with ice, compression, elevation, and rest. For first and second degree sprains, try to elevate the hand as much as possible during the first 24 hours, keeping the hand and finger in a splint. After 48 hours, you can begin heat treatments by soaking your hand in a basin of water a few times a day for the first five days. Range of motion exercises in the hot water will help you regain normal functioning of the fingers gently, as the water

supports the joint. Eventually you can tape the sprained finger to the finger next to it, but be careful to avoid taping the knuckle. A grade three tear usually requires more serious intervention through surgery.

The Torso

THE LOWER BACK—Injuries to the lower back involve the bones and ligaments of the lumbar spine and the bottom five vertebral cushions known as "discs." Mogul skiers experience lower back pain after training on exceptionally hard snow, or irregularly formed moguls. Certainly, the lower back assumes a great deal of pressure during absorption in the moguls, when the knees retract up and in front of the chest. Similarly, aerialists repeatedly drop to the ground from various heights with the force of their body weight and gravity absorbed by the knees and the lumbars of the spine. Ballet skiers, who lift their body weight and perform twisting maneuvers again and again throughout a training session, too, are dependent on the strong muscles of the lower back.

BACK STRAIN—A strain is a muscle tissue tear. If you tear a muscle in the lower back, there is bleeding and swelling into the area of the injury; and again, in a reflex action, the muscles tighten up to prevent the back from moving, reducing the chance of further damage. When you strain the back, it's possible to pinpoint the tear by the swelling and tenderness to the touch. You should ice this area as soon as possible, continuing this treatment for the first 48 hours. This will inhibit extra blood from rushing to the site of the injury, making the spot easier to "flush out" during the healing process. Follow this cold treatment with direct heat after 48 hours. As with a ligament tear, the split in the muscle will fill in with scar tissue. This can take anywhere from five days to three weeks, depending on the extent of the damage.

S.I. JOINT INJURY—The S.I. joint is the point at which the pelvis attaches to the back. It bears great stress during up and down motions (moguls), when pressure needs to be absorbed from below (aerials), and somewhat less in twisting movements (ballet). Landing from any "in-air"movement in ballet, moguls, or in aerials (especially with side-to-side twisting involved) may injure this important stress and weight bearing joint. Pain and swelling are to the side of the "tailbone," where it joins the lower back. Rest and support, such as lying on the floor or on a bed board, and later heat to the area, are immensely helpful. This injury may require many days to heal.

CHRONIC LOW BACK PAIN—Lower back pain is not always the result of an error in technique or rough snow conditions, but can result from secondary minor irregularities in bone formation attributable to heredity (genetics). Individual differences in body symmetry can cause irritation to the lower back, as the body innately compensates for the abnormality. For example, if one leg is significantly longer than the other (more than one-half inch difference), the spine compensates for the tilt in the pelvis, bowing or curving away from the short leg. This can put uneven pressure on the "long legged" side of the spine, causing significant discomfort. Since your center of gravity rests in the pelvis area, tipping can create gross problems in ski technique. What can help correct this irreversible condition? Canting can! "Cants" or wedges are put under the skier's bindings to help him assume a more natural position on the ski, and ultimately, the edge. It's also possible to cant the sole of the boot itself, if the change is within one or two degrees. Cant testing is available at local ski shops and boot factories. Another alternative is to insert corrective lifts in the ski boot, as you would in a running shoe. This should be done under the guidance of a professional.

The Hip and Groin

"HIP POINTER"—An abrupt ski fall onto your side on icy terrain can bruise the bony part of the pelvis that points away from the body, called the iliac crest. This area will become stiff and sore, and the motions required when skiing will be painful. The tendons at-tached to the crest can be torn by the blow, and can take up to three weeks to heal because of their poor blood supply. You should ice the area for 20 minutes, twice a day, for the first 48 hours, and then apply heat for 30 minutes, three times a day, until the pain begins to subside. After a week you can begin to increase your activity level, being careful not to reinjure the crest.

GROIN PULL—Ligaments, tendons, nerves, and blood vessels lie in the inguinal area, where the leg attaches to the pelvis. These structures are subject to "pull," or extreme stretch with sudden or excessive degrees of motion (unexpected, and therefore, uncompensated for). This type of strain can feel like a sudden twinge during a movement, or discomfort and weakness can appear after your activity has stopped. If you can catch this early, applying ice, pressure, and rest for at least 48 hours, you can expedite healing. You should not resume activity until the pain has disappeared from the groin area. Whirlpools or ultrasound are proper forms of therapy, in addition to gradual stretching.

GREATER TROCHANTER INJURY—This part of the upper leg bone, known as the femur, projects sideways and is subject to direct injury, especially in a fall on a hard surface. The ligaments that attach to the area and the bone covering are directly bruised. This too is a contusion and should be treated as such, with ice, rest, anti-inflammatories, and gentle stretching. These may take a long time to heal because of their poor blood supply.

The Upper Leg

PULLED QUADRICEPS—It's easy to pick out a skier in the summertime; the muscles of their upper legs, known as the quadriceps, are strong and well developed. This affects their gait, which is tight, powerful, and deliberate. The impression of power is lasting, and well it should be, for the four muscles which comprise the quadriceps are the largest and strongest in the body. Most quadriceps pulls happen because the muscle was not properly warmed up before being asked to

react quickly. A skier is more likely to experience a tear in these muscles during dry land training, rather than skiing. These tears are classified in degrees, like sprains. Grade one is the least serious, with pain localized over an area the size of a half dollar. Grade three represents an actual gap in the muscle tissue. Like most other muscle tears, there is sudden discomfort which subsides and then returns after a few hours. As the blood from the tear fills the immediate area of the injury, the pain and swelling increase. Ice on and off for the first 48 hours, then begin heat treatments twice a day for 20 minutes using a whirlpool, bath, or hydrocollator, if available.

PULLED HAMSTRING—The hamstring is responsible for bending the knee backward. When you perform a backscratcher, you're shortening the hamstrings, and bringing your heels up in back of your body towards your buttocks. The quadriceps and the hamstrings oppose each other; if the quadricep overpowers the hamstring, the hamstring tears. It can also tear when you haven't stretched properly. As a skier, if you pull this muscle, it will probably be during running events in dry land training. When a hamstring is pulled, the muscles which run down the back of the leg usually tear where they feed into the tendon leading to the pelvic region. This area of tear is most commonly located about one third of the way down the back of the thigh. Apply ice and a compression wrap to the hamstring as soon as possible. After icing three times, for 20 minutes the first day, you can begin heat treatments a few times a day to increase circulation and expedite healing. Moderate pulls can take a week to heal while severe ones can put you out for up to three weeks. When returning to regular training, you should have the thigh wrapped by a trainer; this will reduce any lingering discomfort.

The Lower Leg

DAMAGE TO THE KNEE LIGAMENT—There are two ligaments which run outside of the knee called the medial (inside) and lateral (outside) collateral ligaments; two which cross in the center of the knee joint between the femur and the tibia, called the anterior and posterior cruciate ligaments; and three other minor ligaments. These enable the joint to function like a hinge, while remaining stable at the same time. When the knee is overextended and the ligament is pulled beyond its elasticity level, it tears, either in the middle or at either end where it attaches to the bone. Knee ligament strains are classified into three categories, grade one, which is a slight tear; grade two, a tear or fraying in more than one place along the ligament; and grade three, which is a complete severing of the ligament. The ligaments help stabilize the knee joint, and depending on the severity of the tear, it can be quite painful. Usually it takes about 30 minutes before the swelling begins. Because swelling makes it difficult to test the knee joint for damage, you should try to have your knee examined within this grace period. However, if this is not possible, you can be tested under some form of anesthesia. Grade one tears usually put the athlete out for a week. The knee will be a little swollen and tender when tested. It should be wrapped with an Ace bandage for three days, while icing and elevating as much as possible to reduce swelling. After five days, begin range of motion exercises in the whirlpool. With a grade two sprain, the same care is taken, however it's necessary to use crutches for a week, and the compression bandage should be kept on for five days. A grade two sprain can take up to three weeks to heal, and even then, it is not unusual to experience slight discomfort for months after the injury. A grade three tear, in which the ligament is torn in half, requires surgery as soon as possible and a long, difficult rehabilitation period. A large percentage of these tears happen to the anterior cruciate ligament, but any of the others can be involved. The tear results from a great force placed on the ligament, a force stronger than the ligament itself. Surgery is performed to stitch the ligament back together, and partial immobilization is required. There are varying medical opinions on the precise type and degree of immobilization and rehabilitation treatment required.

KNEE CARTILAGE TEAR—The bones of the upper and lower leg meet in the knee joint area. Without some sort of cushioning, the surface of the femur would wear against the tibia, possibly causing arthritis. Within the knee joint, lying between the two bones, are the medial and lateral meniscus. These are crescent shaped fibro-cartilage which help the joint absorb shock, and stabilize the knee. The menisci look rather like the "pearly," whitish end of a chicken leg; they are equally as smooth, allowing the bones to slide by one another without friction. These menisci are contoured to the surface of the tibia, like a gasket. When the tibia is anchored to the ground, and great force is placed on the femur, the tibia, femur, and menisci lie flush. If the upper body is twisted, the surface of the femur twists as it lies tight against the menisci, and this can tear the cartilage. Unfortunately, cartilage has no blood supply, and in most cases, when it is torn it must be removed. After the meniscus tears, the knee will feel unstable. It fills with synovial fluid, which makes it difficult to bend. The pain will usually be localized over the part of the meniscus that has torn. If a piece of the cartilage has dislodged into the joint, it can lock the motion of the knee. With small tears, you can return to normal activity after a week. With more serious tears, it's necessary to remove the cartilage surgically, otherwise it can rub away at the surfaces of the bones. Nowadays, this can be done microsurgically, in an operation called arthroscopy. After this procedure, it's possible to walk within a day, and full recovery can come within three to four weeks.

KNEECAP DEGENERATION—The kneecap or patella,

is lined along the underside by cartilage. With overuse, or trauma compounded by a possible genetic predisposition to degeneration, this cartilage can soften or wear down, causing pain. In a young person, this type of degeneration is called "chondromalacia." You will notice pain over the kneecap when climbing stairs, or when squatting or kneeling; these movements employ the quadriceps muscle, which pulls the kneecap up and over the femur along a groove. Another indication is "noise" or "crepitus" which you can hear, and feel, if you place your hand over the front of the knee, and bend the leg through full range of motion. If the kneecap is extremely rough, it's possible to have its surface scraped surgically, and one can recover within three weeks. An alternative to surgery is rest for up to six weeks.

KNEE BURSITIS—The knee joint is one of the locations in the body which has bursa sacs. If you recall, these sacs contain a yellowish, slippery fluid that cushions the joint, making it possible for skin, tendons, and bone to slide effortlessly and comfortably. Fourteen such sacs are found in the knee. If you fall or cut your knee, you can break open any number of these sacs. There are different types of bursitis, some in front of the kneecap, underneath, or in the back of the knee. Fluid leaks out of the sac and a bubble forms underneath the skin, inhibiting normal range of motion and causing pain. Icing a few times a day for 20 minutes and two aspirin at mealtimes should be tried first. If this treatment fails, it is sometimes necessary to drain the sac, inject it with cortisone, and then wear an Ace bandage for 48 hours to keep the sac from swelling.

SHIN SPLINTS—An aching in the front of a skier's lower leg could be shin splints, boot bang, or a stress fracture. It would be difficult to develop shin splints from skiing itself, because the boots immobilize the muscles to a large degree. Still, it does occur. If you are complementing on-snow training with running, the pain you're experiencing may very well be shin splints. This pain can be caused by a rip in the anterior tibial muscle, inflammation of the bone covering along the tibia, poor blood supply to the shin muscles (peroneals

and anterior tibial), or a tiny crack, called a stress fracture, in the tibia. Shin splints usually develop from overuse, most commonly during early season running. If the problem is muscle related, with continual use and little regard for the pain, the symptoms can become worse and the muscle can actually tear away from the bone. The quickest way to recover is to rest for a week, ice the injury twice a day for 20 minutes during the first 48 hours, follow with heat, and take anti-inflammatories to reduce the swelling. A trainer can advise you about taping and heel lifts. With a stress fracture, the pain will be localized, usually just below the top third of the tibia where the bone tapers. In this case, there is little you can do but rest for three to four weeks.

In the animal world in general, it seems to be a general biological rule that the heart rate varies inversely with the size of the species. For example, the canary has a rate of approximately 1,000, the elephant, in the neighborhood of about twenty-five beats per minute.

RICHARD H. STRAUSS

BOOT BANG OR BOOT BRUISE—The front of the shin is extremely vulnerable to bruising because of the lack of padding from either muscle or fat tissues, which tend to dissipate the shock of a blow. The bone covering, otherwise known as the periosteum, can become inflamed with repeated injury to the tissues. Boot bang seems to be most common in aerial and mogul skiing, where repeated force is placed on the front of the shin as it presses against the tongue of the boot. This can be severely painful, and the pain may inhibit normal ski technique. A few remedies besides rest are available.

Pad the tongue of the ski boot with foam. This ought to smooth out any pressure points which may be compounding the problem. If you must compete, have the shin taped as you would for a shin split, and take a few aspirin. This reduces the discomfort. Ice the shin a few times a day, and soak it in a whirlpool if you have the facilities.

ANKLE FRACTURE—With the advent of higher boots and multidirectional release bindings, the incidence of ankle injuries has diminished significantly over the past 10 years, while an increase of knee injuries has developed. This is the topic of great debate: some sports medicine professionals argue that knee injuries have not increased, but that it is our ability to diagnose them that has become more sophisticated. At any rate, ankle injuries still occur, despite the protective skeleton of the ski boot. Ankle injuries in skiing can happen when tremendous pressure is transferred from the foot to the knob of the ankle joint. An ankle fracture is remarkable painful. You'll be unable to bear weight on the joint, which usually begins to swell within an hour of the injury. While you're waiting to be seen by a professional, put a bag of ice along the surface of the ankle and hold it there by wrapping an Ace bandage around it. Immobilize the area with a splint if possible, and raise the foot above your heart to reduce swelling. Depending on the extent of the damage, you could be in a cast up to three months. The ankle will be quite stiff once out of the cast, and physical therapy is a must.

BUNIONS AND BUNIONETTES—Continual use of ski boots can lead to pressure points along the toe area. A bunion from a tight boot will develop on the joint of the big toe; a bunionette will develop on the joint of the little toe. The pressure from the boot tends to push the big or little toe in toward the others, and can sometimes cause problems across nearby toes as well. The base of these toes can become quite painful, swollen, and covered with a thick layer of skin. A sensitive area along the foot can affect your ski technique; the pain may cause you to subconsciously tense the body each time the ski chatters, instead of absorbing the shock. Though this may appear to be a trivial physical problem, you can imagine the serious effects that it can have on your skiing. It's possible to have the shell of the boot heated and "pushed out" away from this sensitive area, thus relieving pressure and reducing friction. Another thing you can try is placing a soft pad between the toe with the bunion or bunionette and the neighboring toe to help realign them. While it is still in the painful stage, ice it each day for 20 minutes, and take two aspirin at mealtimes to reduce swelling.

Madeline Üvhaggn—SWED, Hayley Wolff—U.S.A., Catherine Frarier—FRA

DORSAL EXOSTOSIS—Like bunions, a bump on the top of the foot can develop from the friction of the foot against the top of the ski boot. This bony deposit can be very painful. To relieve the pain, you must ease the pressure over this spot. You can do this a couple of ways . . . by cutting into the tongue of the ski boot and removing some of the "stuffing" that helps tighten the fit of the boot, or by placing a doughnut, a round foam pad with a hole in the center, directly over the bump.

BONE SPURS—Exostosis, a bony outgrowth from the bone, may occur in any pressure area on the bone. Skiers usually get these bone deposits somewhere along the foot, due to ill fitting boots. The pressure stimulates the overproduction of osteoblasts, or bone cells, which deposit over the area of pressure. The result is a bony deposit, or bump, which can be quite painful. Discomfort may be relieved by refitting your boots (pushing the shell out over the raised area), or applying a dressing such as a doughnut. Bone spurs may take a summer season to go away. They resorb slowly, and generally do not require surgery.

TOE BANG—In ballet skiing many of the maneuvers are initiated by pressing off the toes, and some landings are taken with considerable force along the front of the ski and boot. These repetitive motions can force the toes against the front or top of the boot and bruise them. This also occurs in mogul skiing when the lines are deep and the snow is hard, because you have to press through the turn as well as sit back a little more than normal. This raises the toes hard against the top, or front, of the boot as your try to brake yourself. Usually, the big toe is the most painful. The bruise feels like a minor sprain, and if your activity level is not reduced, you can lose the toenail as well. You should ice the injury a few times a day and stop skiing until it is no longer painful when in the boot. If you must compete, aspirin will reduce your discomfort, and taping sometimes supports the toe enough to ease the pain. If you've developed a black toenail from toe jamming the front of the boot, you can reduce pain by relieving pressure from underneath the nail, provided you catch the problem within the first 48 hours. Heat a pin or paper clip until it is red hot, and then press the tip against the center of the nail. The hole in the nail will release pressure created from the build up of blood under the nail. If the nail has been bruised for a few days, tape it to the toe for a couple of weeks, until the nail underneath has a chance to harden. Otherwise, it can be really uncomfortable.

Cold Exposure

Skiers spend most of the day out in the cold, and should be informed about injuries specific to long and short periods of exposure to low temperatures. The design of ski boots alone predisposes the skier to frostbite. The wind on the face and the sweat produced by vigorous activity in the cold can present tricky heat retention problems.

When you shiver out in the cold, your muscles are working to heat the body; in fact, 75 percent of the energy used for muscle work goes to heating the body. Shivering can increase heat production by 500 percent for short periods of time. Heat is lost from the body in four ways: conduction (when you sit on the snow waiting for the starter to call your name, your body heat is being conducted, or transferred, to the snow), convection (as you ski through the air and when the wind blows across your face, heat from your skin is lost), radiation (when you ski without a hat, a high percentage of heat is lost from the vascular areas of the head and neck), and evaporation (when you sweat or breathe, heat evaporates).

Hypothermia results when the body's heat loss exceeds its heat production, causing its core temperature to drop below 35 degrees C, or 95 degrees F. Prolonged exposure to cold causes hypothermia. In skiing, mild cases (core temperature above 35 degrees C) are caused when a skier takes a fall and must wait for help, or when one gets lost, which can happen on glaciers in Europe during a "white-out." A person experiencing hypothermia may gradually have trouble with coordination, taking ill care to cover up from the cold, and may become increasingly lethargic. Cover the person up as soon as possible, and once inside,

"rewarm" him by heating the torso with blankets and hot water bottles. In more severe cases, loss of vision, slurred speech, urination, stupor, and possibly coma may result. Lifting these individuals should be done with great care. Any physical, biological, or chemical changes can send the heart into fibrillation, therefore, these individuals should be treated as delicately as someone with a spine injury.

One of the most common cold injuries is frostbite. Some cases of frostbite are predisposed by tight garments, contact with metal, wet skin, previous frostbite, and cigarette smoking. When frostnip or frostbite sets in, the blood vessels in the affected area constrict, while the veins dilate. As the tissue begins to freeze, ice crystals form between or within the cells and may eventually destroy the cell. When the skin is frostnipped, it does not appear white, but is very firm, and free of sensation. A frostbitten area will look whitish, while feeling hard, cold, and insensitive. Frostnip involves ears, nose, cheeks, toes, and fingers, and can be treated by placing a warm hand against the area, blowing warm breath on the spot, or placing hands or toes under the armpit. Superficial frostbite is hard and waxy looking. Upon thawing, the area will feel numb, followed by a burning sensation. Both can result in blisters and discoloration of the affected area.

The Aches and Pains Associated with Travel

A few problems which you may encounter while traveling and competing are not a direct result of working the skis back and forth across the snow. The Regional, National, and most of all World Cup teams have rigorous schedules at the height of the ski season, almost always demanding travel across long distances. For instance, the World Cup Team tours through Europe for two months during the winter, stopping in a different country each week. Not only can the trip to Europe create discomfort due to respiratory problems and time change, but sometimes the change in cuisine from week to week can upset the intestinal system. Stress, which is an integral part of competition, can disrupt

sleeping and eating patterns, which in turn can produce mood changes, and affect performance. These discomforts are a little less tangible than a dislocated shoulder or shin splints, but they are every bit as real, and every bit as uncomfortable.

Despite all of the horror stories you hear about missed flights, problems associated with handling 25 ski bags weighing 50 pounds apiece, lost bags, passports, traveler's checks, and people, and metal detectors that alarm every security person in the airport to come running with the handcuffs because somebody on the team packed a tuning kit in the carry-on luggage . . . despite all of this, traveling by air with an athletic ski team can be a wonderful experience! But the warm feeling of camaraderie can be overshadowed by minor physical discomforts, which in turn can make a trip of a few hours seem like days.

If you're traveling with a cold, the change in cabin air pressure in the plane can cause great discomfort, especially in the Eustachian tube of the ears, which may become further blocked. If you have a respiratory infection, take a nasal decongestant before flying. This will open the blocked Eustachian tube, equalizing the air pressure in the middle ear with that of the cabin. If you are on the plane and don't have a decongestant, try plugging your nose with the thumb and forefinger of one hand, and force air out of your mouth in short bursts, saying the letter "E-E-E-E-E!" a number of times. This, too, should help unplug the ears.

If you are traveling by air over several time zones, upon reaching your destination you will probably experience "jet lag." Your thinking patterns and physical performance may be substandard for a few days, and your sleep patterns may be disrupted as well. If jet lag is coupled with the need to acclimatize to a higher altitude, those sleepless nights may be accentuated by dizziness and mild headache. Obviously, you should begin training slowly these first few days. If your decision-making ability is impaired, the split second reactions which you rely on to perform your maneuvers safely are late. A few extra hours of rest may prevent a season of recuperation due to injury. Quell that urge to get out there and attack the courses. Instead, shorten your training hours by breaking the day into sections, and

get plenty of rest between sessions. Jet lag varies from person to person, but usually lasts a couple of days; the more time zones you cross, the longer the side effects seem to last.

Another side effect, known as "traveler's diarrhea" may be experienced for the first few days which is caused by a bacterium (Escherichia coli) in the intestinal tract. Serious cases are accompanied by nausea, vomiting, and dehydration, and require a physician's attention. You may experience mild cases of diarrhea, such as a few loose bowel movements, caused by the jet lag which upsets the biological clock, or by a change in diet. If you take the time to pack a few things before you begin your trip, you can treat these mild cases yourself. A bottle of Pepto-Bismol, some ampicillin, or a dose of tetracycline (five 500-mg capsules) are recommended, as well as frequently drinking small amounts of fluid. Caffeine, alcohol, and aspirin should be avoided. In European countries such as Italy, Spain, France, and Greece, you should drink bottled water. If you're unsure whether to drink the water in a certain area, watch what other travelers are doing; if everyone is ordering mineral water, it's a safe bet that you should do the same.

At some competitions, ski teams stay in villages that are considerably lower than the altitude at which they compete; they drive up to the ski area in the mornings. This practice may affect a few of the athletes adversely, resulting in acute mountain sickness (AMS). AMS symptoms may include headache, vomiting, weakness, sleep disturbance, or lethargy. Such manifestations are the side effects of a depletion of oxygen in the cells of the body. There are a few different theories on the physiological effects of oxygen depletion, one of which is that oxygen in the cells helps balance the concentration of salt, and therefore, water within the cell. A depletion of oxygen increases the concentration of sodium within the cell, which in turn signals the body to send water into that area. As water rushes to the site, the cell swells, affecting areas which are responsible for headache, nausea, and the like.

Appendices

F.I.S. Mogul Course Standards

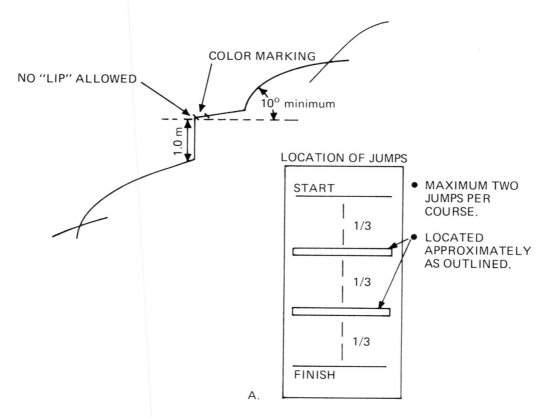

COLOR MARKING

NO "LIP" ALLOWED

10° minimum

1.0 m

LOCATION OF JUMPS

START

1/3

1/3

1/3

FINISH

A.

● MAXIMUM TWO JUMPS PER COURSE.

● LOCATED APPROXIMATELY AS OUTLINED.

OPTIONAL JUMPS IN THE MOGUL COURSE

F.I.S. Mogul Course Standards

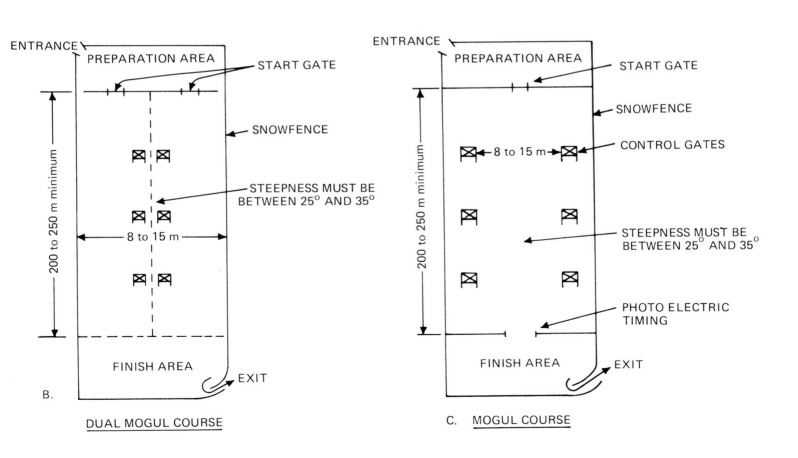

B. DUAL MOGUL COURSE

C. MOGUL COURSE

Moguls Layout
F.I.S. Course Standard

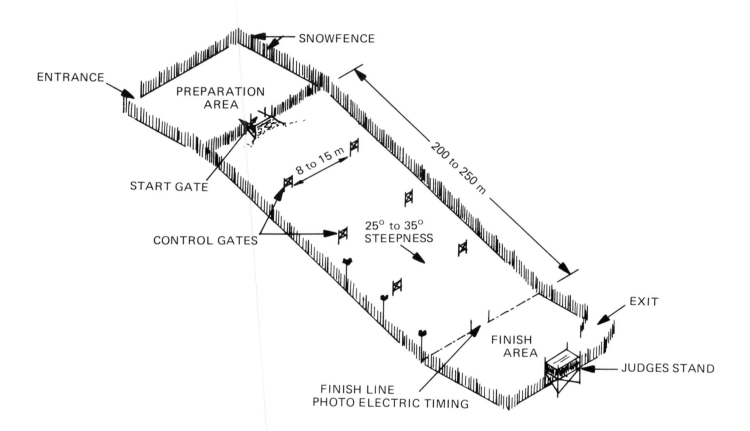

NOTE: U.S.S.A. MOGUL COURSE STANDARDS VARY SLIGHTLY: 20-35 M WIDE

Aerial Layout
F.I.S. Course Standard

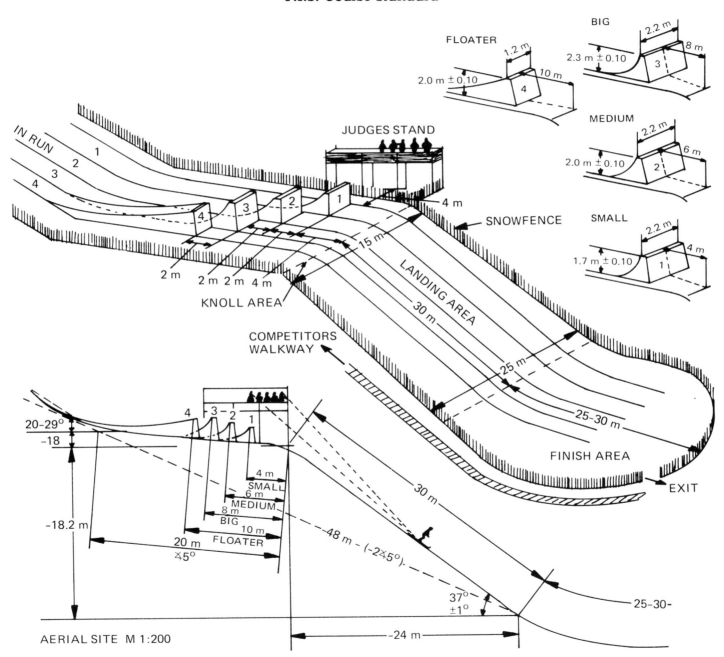

FLOATER
1.2 m
2.0 m ± 0.10
10 m
4

BIG
2.2 m
2.3 m ± 0.10
8 m
3

MEDIUM
2.2 m
2.0 m ± 0.10
6 m
2

SMALL
2.2 m
1.7 m ± 0.10
4 m
1

JUDGES STAND

IN RUN
1
2
3
4

4
3
2
1

4 m

SNOWFENCE

15 m

2 m   2 m 2 m 4 m

KNOLL AREA

LANDING AREA

30 m

25 m

25-30 m

COMPETITORS
WALKWAY

FINISH AREA

EXIT

30 m

20-29°
-18
-18.2 m

4 3 2 1

4 m
SMALL
6 m
MEDIUM
8 m
BIG
10 m
FLOATER

20 m
∡5°

48 m - (-2∡5°)

37°
±1°

25-30-

-24 m

AERIAL SITE M 1:200

Ballet Layout
F.I.S. Course Standard

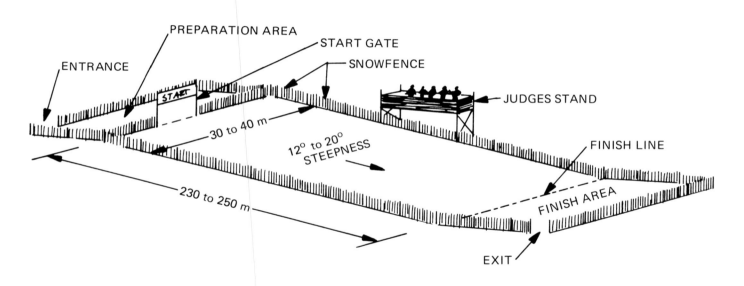

NOTE: U.S.S.A. BALLET STANDARDS VARY SLIGHTLY: 10°–16° STEEPNESS
200–250M LENGTH